Right or Wrong?

Essays in Moral Theology

RIGHT OR WRONG?

Essays in Moral Theology

Patrick Hannon

VERITAS

First published 2009 by
Veritas Publications
7/8 Lower Abbey Street
Dublin 1
Ireland
Email publications@veritas.ie
Website www.veritas.ie

ISBN 978 1 84730 129 1

10 9 8 7 6 5 4 3 2 1

Scripture references taken from the New Revised Standard Version
Bible, copyright © 1989, Division of Christian Education of the
National Council of the Churches in the USA.

Designed by Barbara Croatto
Printed in the Republic of Ireland by ColourBooks Ltd, Dublin

Veritas books are printed on paper made from the wood pulp of
managed forests. For every tree felled, at least one tree is planted,
thereby renewing natural resources.

Contents

Introduction   7

1. Was I Right?   13

2. Can Gay Men Be Priests?   21

3. Four Half-Truths and a Lie   31

4. Child Sexual Abuse: Some Rules for the Debate   41

5. Justice Tempered by Love   53

6. Human Rights and Christian Faith   71

7. Christian Values in a Pluralist Society   85

8. Sharia?   101

9. No Catholic Need Apply?   109

10. Aquinas, Morality and Law   123

11. 'Wragg is in Custody': A Court Case Observed   137

Acknowledgements   149

Introduction

Someone is said to have remarked that he (or she) would rather have a moral problem than a real one. I don't know whether the quip's perpetrator had in mind the manufactured dilemmas found in textbooks of moral philosophy or theology, some of which seem very unreal indeed, or whether the gibe merely voices the scepticism of the practical person about the usefulness of any kind of theory. Or – what would of course be serious – does it betoken an idea of morality in which it is seen as something rarefied or incidental, rather than as part of the warp and woof of everyone's everyday life?

The problems posed by those who people the vignettes in this book's opening chapter are real, and the people are real, if here well disguised for confidentiality's sake: a girl uncertain of the respective weight of the claims of friendship and moral conviction; parents torn between love of a son or daughter and loyalty to teachings that seem central in the traditions in which they were brought up; a priest caught in tensions generated by his various roles. Real also are the people and the problems that in a different way are the concern of Chapters 2, 3 and 4: a gay man pondering a vocation to the priesthood; the plight of someone for whom a love-relationship has meant exclusion from the Eucharist; the suffering of one who has been marked for life by sexual abuse.

The issues with which the following chapters deal – human rights, Catholic social teaching, Christian values in a pluralist society – are among the moral issues which, for all the swiftness of change today, remain live in the

Catholic Church and in Ireland, and indeed, in an image that is becoming worn but isn't far-fetched, in the modern global village. There are new neighbours in our part of the village of course: Mosc Átha Cliath is no longer the only house of worship of Allah in Dublin, and Islam is the second most numerous religion in the country of the eldest Daughter of the Church. So it can be hoped that a chapter on Sharia won't be thought out of place.

Although the 2008 US presidential election is over, with a result that has been welcomed throughout the world, the themes treated in Chapter 9 will surface again, in Ireland and in other countries of the European Union as well as in the United States. However, US debate about the role of religious conviction in politics has a special significance in Catholic theology, for the thinking that most decisively shaped the Declaration on Religious Freedom of the Second Vatican Council originated in the experience of the Church in the US. The debate among Catholics themselves has sometimes been acrimonious, regrettably if to some extent understandably (the stakes are high); but it has yielded valuable clarification of ideas that are critical to constructive interchange in a religiously pluralist society.

It cannot be said – although it sometimes is – that the Council's teaching on religious freedom is an obvious outcome of inherited teaching about Church–State relations, and about morality and law and religion. A mere ten years or so earlier, the chief architect of the *Declaration*, John Courtney Murray SJ, had been silenced for his writings on precisely these themes. Murray's thought was progressive, to be sure, but many of the ideas that he worked with were available in theological tradition. Chapter 10 here is included to show that, for all that the context in which Aquinas wrote is a world long gone, the method of his theologising foreign to us, his thinking may still stimulate creative thought about morality, politics and law today.

Finally, there's 'Wragg is in Custody', a piece whose genre may make its inclusion in a moral theology book surprising. Its reappearance is in fact partly meant to illustrate (as in a different way the chapter on Aquinas) that moral theology can take many forms, an idea that we may be more at home with now than when the piece first appeared. Of course, what it chiefly calls to mind is the shocking truth that human rights can be violated, and in the name of justice and the law, by the very institutions whose *raison d'être* is to protect them: something that in succeeding decades we have become familiar with nearer home: think of Nicky Kelly, for example; the Tallaght Two; Nora Wall; and Ireland's part in the wrongdoing that is symbolised by Guantanamo Bay.

The vindication of the Birmingham Six and the Guildford Four (to mention only those that in the end received most public attention) was achieved painfully slowly, after tireless campaigning by people on this island and that of our neighbour. Most of the campaigners are nameless, people with no pretensions, women and men for whom it was enough to know that a great wrong had been done, and who were determined that it should be set right. They included people for whom religion meant little or nothing, some perhaps for whom the Churches are part of the systems in which injustice can go unchecked. However, they included also, and importantly, people whose inspiration was Jesus and his teaching, and a Gospel that empowers disciples to care for prisoners, and to work for justice and freedom. They included Tomas O'Fiaich, Basil Hume and Bishop Edward Daly of Derry, and the priests Raymond Murray and Denis Faul, Bobby Gilmore and Joe Taaffe, and Sister Sarah Clarke: a reminder of the role that may still be played by leaders of the Churches and their institutions.

Mindful of the warning implicit in my opening anecdote, I hope the reader will accept that thinking about moral problems from the standpoint of a theology isn't an idle pursuit. How useful the reflections collected here is another matter, of course. In selecting them I had in mind not just students of theology, or people who may be professionally interested, but a general reader, interested still, or puzzled, or irritated, by the persistence of ideas about living that come out of a Christian tradition. Writing that is 'occasional' gives at best a fragmentary picture, but I hope that these fragments earn their place.

A theology? A Christian tradition? The indefinite article will already have put off – perhaps incensed – a reader of a certain turn of mind. Isn't this a book about *Catholic* moral theology, as was said a few paragraphs back, and as can be gleaned from skimming the contents? Yes, but there is much in Catholic theology that, shared as it is with the other Christian traditions, is better described by the word 'Christian'; and there are other Christian traditions. For that matter, there *are* several Catholic traditions, something which may also be glimpsed in what is offered here.

At another place on the spectrum of readers is someone who is impatient at the suggestion that there is any reflection to be done in the Catholic Church. The teaching of the Church is clear, such a person might say, meaning the teaching of the Church's Magisterium; and, for the faithful, debate is out of the question. This reaction is found among people of a so-called traditionalist mind set, though it can be found also among disciples of the *enfants terribles* of the moment, Messrs Hitchens, Dawkins and Harris, for whom anything less than a frank dogmatism can only be dangerous hypocrisy.

'The teaching of the Church is clear': well, yes and no. Yes, there are clear principles in the repertoire of ideas that Christian tradition has handed on for the guidance of conscience. They feature in the teaching of catechisms, in encyclicals of the popes and the statements of episcopal conferences; and they include permanent and unvarying reminders of the requirements of faithful discipleship of Christ, as a glance at almost any of this book's chapters will show. However, there are also principles and ideas whose application in practice may vary, as circumstances vary, as again may be seen in Chapters 5, 6, 7, 9 and 10.

It is sometimes said that Church leaders and theologians have complicated a simple message, the message that God is love, and that we are invited and enabled to love God in return, and enjoined to show that love by loving our neighbour. Or, as it is also said, we should follow and imitate Jesus Christ, incarnation both of God's love and of the love to which Christians are called, and that if we do so we will be doing 'the one thing necessary'.

The Christian Gospel is indeed about love, and whenever it is reduced to legalistic moralising – or any kind of moralising for that matter – it is misrepresented. However, the announcement of the Gospel is also a call to conversion, to 'let your manner of life be worthy of the Gospel of Christ', as the letter to the Philippians has it. From the outset, preachers and teachers of the Word saw a need to list attitudes and behaviours that befit or do not befit a faithful disciple of Jesus.

A moral pedagogy that confined itself to generalities, that avoided engagement with application of principle to practice and failed to address the varying circumstances in which Christians live out their lives – such a pedagogy would leave the conscientious questioner short. That is why Catholic moral teaching and theological reflection are characteristically disposed to offer a more concrete guidance, in which attention to circumstances is prominent and which recognise that, as the saying goes, circumstances alter cases, even as they insist that there are acts and attitudes which to a Christian can never be right.

Anyone who takes even minimal interest will know that recent decades have been turbulent for the Churches and their leaders, and especially for Catholic teaching and the practice of moral theology. This too may be glimpsed in the pieces collected here; indeed it is because of it that some of the problems take the shape they have taken, both the personal moral questions and the more general. On the whole though, I have chosen to concentrate on what can be said with some assurance, and relatively uncontroversially, whilst mindful of the dangers of simplification. There is no future for certainties that are contrived, nor should honest questions go unheard or debate be stifled as it tries to get to truth. However, sometimes it is possible – and for practical or 'pastoral' purposes desirable – to put controverted matters to one side and to see what in any case may be agreed.

Most of the chapters appeared first in *The Furrow*, and I thank Ronan Drury for permission to reproduce them here. Thanks also to Dermot Lane and Columba Press; Chapter 7, updated as necessary, is from their *New Century, New Society*; to Margaret Burns who with Pauline Berwick, under the auspices of the Council for Social Welfare, organised a study day and edited a book entitled *The Rights of the Child*, from which Chapter 6 comes; to Michael Conway, editor of the *IrishTheological Quarterly*, in which the paper from which chapter 10 is adapted first appeared; and to Eoin Cassidy (editor) and Veritas for allowing re-publication of 'Justice Tempered by Love', from *The Common Good in an Unequal World*.

I owe special thanks to Ruth Kennedy and Caitriona Clarke of Veritas for editorial expertise (not to mention patience), and to commissioning editor Donna Doherty for her encouragement.

1.
Was I Right?

A young woman is perplexed. Her friend, aged eighteen, is going to England for an abortion. She is terrified at the prospect but is convinced that it is her only course. Can the young woman, herself convinced that abortion is wrong, accompany her friend? She has tried to dissuade her, has offered to help her in any other way she can. She feels she should stand by her (she is the only one who knows), but she is torn between her belief about abortion and her sense of compassion for the plight of her friend.

A father and mother are distressed. Their daughter has told them that she is a lesbian and that her relationship with a friend has reached the stage of physical expression. The parents are conscious of Church teaching about the wrongness of homosexual activity and have tried to persuade their daughter to break off the relationship. While she lives at home there is no realistic possibility of breaking it off, even if she wanted to, which she doesn't. The father wants her to leave home and take a job in another place. Her mother is less sure. Both believe that what she is doing is wrong. Neither parent wants to alienate their daughter or cause her to think that they love her any less.

A couple have decided to marry in a registry office. They love each other deeply, are committed to one another, but a Church wedding would mean nothing to them, for they have abandoned religious belief and practice. The young man's parents are distraught. They are active members of their local Catholic Church and their faith means a lot to them. They love their son deeply but cannot in conscience approve of his decision. Should they attend the wedding? The thought of not being there as their son sets out on married life brings heartache, but can they watch him embark upon a course of action which they profoundly believe to be wrong?

Three scenarios which, give or take details, are familiar enough these days, and in each case the people concerned took the path of compassion, with a little help from their pastors. Pressed, they or their pastors might say that such a course was called for by 'common sense' and 'ordinary human feelings'. One of the pastors recalled Catholic theology's principles about cooperation in wrongdoing, and Catholic theology's distinction between what is objectively wrong and what the subjective culpability of a wrongdoer might be. The resolution in each case was felt to have been the right one, although there was a residual sense of unease.

A resolution of dilemmas such as these will never be easy for the kind of person for whom they are dilemmas (there are, of course, people for whom the situations would present no problem at all). They are problems of conscience that must be respected as such. Invocations by a well-intentioned advisor of the priority of 'compassion' and 'ordinary human feelings' are unlikely to make the problem disappear. It *ought* to bite when we are asked to go along with things that are contrary to what we believe to be right.

At one level the cases do raise the question of how far one may cooperate in what one believes to be the wrongdoing of another, and standard principles of moral theology concerning cooperation are in fact helpful here. The heart of the matter is that normally one will not want to cooperate at all, but that there may be circumstances in which, for a sufficient reason, one may cooperate up to a point. Presupposed is that one doesn't formally approve what is happening and that no scandal is caused. But cases such as these give rise to a different line of thought also, and it is this that I wish to explore here.

Underlying dilemmas of this sort is the fact that we find ourselves placed in a variety of roles as regards morality and that these roles are sometimes in tension with one another. The roles overlap, of course, but they are distinguishable. Distinguishing them may help to identify the tensions and discern how the tensions may be lived with, if not always resolved. For brevity, I shall take here the case of a priest, since a priest's case offers the most comprehensive set of possibilities; but I am conscious of the fact that the point may be made, *mutatis mutandis*, of other ministers in the Church, and indeed of people who aren't formally ministers, but who may find themselves involved in situations such as those sketched above.

Roles in relation to morality in which a priest usually finds himself are that of preacher, teacher, confessor and counsellor. There is also a 'prophetic' role in relation to morality and a role of 'witness'; and, of course, even as he exercises any other role, each person is in any case a moral subject, actor or agent. Here our reflections are limited to the first four roles mentioned.

It may be useful to notice at this point that the roles of preacher and teacher might be said to be concerned with 'objective' aspects of morality. The preacher sets out the ideals of Christian morality and exhorts his hearers to take them to heart. The teacher hopes to educate his listeners and, among other things, explains the nature and basis for these ideals and the principles and norms for behaviour that reflect them. You could say that in these roles, especially that of teacher, there is a concern for what is *normative* in the Christian moral inheritance.

The context of the role of confessor or of counsellor is different. Each of these is concerned with a 'subjective' experience of morality, with the way that a particular person or group is managing – or not – to make moral sense in their lives. Each takes the person as he or she is now, and the concern with morality is specific and existential. The confessor is concerned with reconciliation, with mediating God's forgiving and saving grace where moral failure is acknowledged, and there is a will to return to or make a fresh start on the way of the Lord Jesus. The role of counsellor is not here restricted to that of the trained counsellor, and may include the informal sort of assistance and advice proffered to someone who is trying to see straight in a difficult situation or find a way out of a dilemma.

It can easily be seen that there are tensions inherent in combining these roles. A preacher will proclaim the demands of the Christian way; as confessor he is trying to connect with the conscience of someone who knows the demands but hasn't measured up to them. A teacher of Christian morality will be expected to set out clearly the principles that are available in the Christian tradition for the guidance of concrete choice and action. In a counselling role, he or she is trying to help someone discern the moral truth in a particular situation; the concern is with the concrete possibilities for implementing Christian ideals in the circumstances in which an individual now finds himself or herself.

Tensions are inescapable. The preacher or teacher will want to do justice to the vision for good living that the

Christian way provides, and so will want to enunciate ideal or principle firmly and clearly. However, they won't want to do so in a way that will deter or discourage the hearer. The confessor and counsellor will be aware of the complexity of concrete situations, of the fact that people can only do what they are able for, that we all fail, that there is a brokenness about human living which is never finally overcome this side of the fullness of the reign of God. But they may be uneasy about appearing to blur the ideals, water down the demands, make little of imperatives that are essential in the moral message of Christianity.

It may be asked whether theology offers any clue as to priorities in situations such as those described above. Pope John Paul II, in *Reconciliatio et Paenitentia*, adverts to what he calls a fundamental presupposition: 'what is pastoral is not opposed to what is doctrinal. Nor can pastoral action prescind from doctrinal content, from which in fact it draws its substance and real validity.' Can theology help establish priorities when we experience tension between our various roles *vis-à-vis* morality?

A starting point is that Jesus was not in the first place a teacher of normative morality. True, he taught moral norms: he reiterated the Decalogue, making it clear that his message was not intended to abolish but to fulfil the Law; and a glance through the gospels is enough to show that he didn't balk at saying what was right and wrong when the situation called for him to do so. But it is interesting to notice that the proportion of moral teaching, and in particular of normative moral teaching, is small compared to other elements in his preaching and to the general shape of his mission as this is recounted by the evangelists.

For the narratives feature miracles, healing stories and instances of the forgiveness of sin much more than they do moral teaching. The parables, even when they are concerned with morality, are if anything subversive of conventional notions of what the good life is, as when the prodigal's welcome makes the other son wonder about the point of having been dutiful; or when the workers who came at the eleventh hour get the same pay as those who were there all day.

So the proportion of the gospel narratives whose concern is normative morality is relatively small. A similar point can be made about other New Testament books. Paul, for example, spends the greater part of each of his letters reflecting on the great theological themes – sin, redemption, the Law and grace, the resurrection of Jesus, death and eternal life – before turning to moral teaching and exhortation. The letter to the Romans concludes a lengthy reflection on these themes with a paeon: 'O the depth of the riches and wisdom and knowledge of God! How unsearchable his judgements and how inscrutable his ways! ... For from him and through him and to him are all things. To him be glory for ever. Amen' (11:33, 36). And the moral teaching that ensues is introduced as follows: 'I appeal to you therefore, brethren ... to present your bodies as a living sacrifice, holy and acceptable to God, which is your spiritual worship. Do not be conformed to this world but be transformed by the renewal of your mind, that you may prove what is the will of God, what is good and acceptable and perfect' (12:1, 2).

It goes without saying that in the Christian way of life, love of God and love of neighbour are inseparably interconnected. However, it must be said also that 'Gospel' is prior to 'Law', that the proclamation of the Kingdom comes before the call to repentance, that in the end what is distinctive about the Christian vision is its word of a gracious, forgiving and merciful God, revealed in the personal history of Jesus. Witness to the Gospel involves right living, but it involves above all the incarnation of compassion and love in the way of the Lord Jesus.

This insight will not eliminate the tensions inherent in combining the roles of preacher and teacher, confessor and counsellor. It could not obviate the painful process of thinking through dilemmas such as those narrated above, but it provides a starting point and constant point of reference.

2.
Can Gay Men Be Priests?

Can homosexual men be admitted to seminaries and be ordained priests in the Roman Catholic Church? Anyone with ears to hear or eyes to see will know that this question has received an authoritative reply, though opinion is divided on whether the answer is yes or no. The opinion isn't the casual and perhaps untutored reaction of persons in the street but includes the views of cardinals, bishops, seminary officials, theologians, canonists and religious affairs correspondents, not to mention homosexual priests and seminarians.

The diversity of interpretation raises many issues, including the question how an official pronouncement on a matter so grave can leave any doubt as to its meaning. The Instruction[1] was in preparation for some years, and in the six to twelve months before it appeared its contents were regularly the subject of leaks and media discussion: the entire document was leaked to an Italian news agency a week before its official release. There was opportunity for reflection on what it says, therefore, and its framers had an opportunity to resolve ambiguities or other problems with the text. It must be assumed that what we have in the document is the considered verdict of the Congregation for Catholic Education, and it is a verdict which has the approval of Pope Benedict.

A VERDICT
The aim of the Instruction is plainly stated at the outset. It does not intend, it says, to treat all the questions about affectivity and sexuality that arise in connection with seminary formation. 'Rather, it contains norms concerning a

specific question, made more urgent by the current situation, and that is: whether to admit to the seminary and to holy orders candidates who have deep-seated homosexual tendencies.' It recalls essential theology of ministerial priesthood, and Catholic teaching on homosexuality as set out especially in the *Catechism of the Catholic Church*. The essence of its own contribution is that 'the Church, while profoundly respecting the persons in question, cannot admit to the seminary or to holy orders those who practise homosexuality, present deep-seated homosexual tendencies or support the so-called "gay culture"'.

Given Catholic teaching about homosexuality the Instruction's requirements concerning homosexual practice were, of course, to be expected. The notion that a candidate for a celibate priesthood should have established his capacity to live chastely over a period of three or four years is no more strange in the case of a homosexual man than it is in the case of someone who is heterosexual. Nor is it strange that a heterosexual who goes through an actively homosexual phase should be expected to have sorted himself out before undertaking a celibate life.

More difficult is the meaning of the caveat against support for 'gay culture', and there has been debate about the scope of this expression. However, the greatest difficulty by far has been with the import of the exclusion of men with 'deep-seated homosexual tendencies'. For this has been taken by some to refer to the condition of homosexuality, what is sometimes called homosexual orientation; and those who take this line hold that the Instruction excludes homosexuals from the priesthood even if they are chaste.

YES AND NO

The view that it does has been applauded by some commentators, who believe that it heralds a much-needed reform of the priesthood. The opinions of three of these, George Weigel, Joseph Fessio SJ and Richard J. Neuhaus, were given prominence in Anglophone media coverage, not just as well-known commentators on religious affairs in the US but also because each was believed to be especially knowledgeable about the Pope's thinking. The three concurred in the view that, in Weigel's words, 'The document simply reiterates long-standing Catholic teaching and practice ... It's clear that practice slackened ... and the document is calling the Church back to its own discipline of ensuring that a man before ordination is psychologically, spiritually and emotionally capable of living this very demanding lifestyle'.[2] All agreed also that the Instruction teaches that homosexual orientation disqualifies a man from ordination.

A startling expression of this viewpoint was provided by Richard Neuhaus, editor-in-chief of the respected *First Things*.[3]

> Those who have been afflicted [sic] by [same sex attraction] but have been chastely celibate protest that the instruction cannot possibly mean that, were they candidates for ordination today, they should be refused. But that is precisely what the instruction seems to say. That does not mean they cannot continue as good and faithful priests. Most certainly it does not in any way throw into question the validity of their priesthood and therefore the validity of the sacraments they administer. But it would seem to mean that they should not have been ordained in the first place, and those with a similar lack of 'affective maturity' should not be ordained in the future.[4]

The logic of this is perhaps not obvious but at any rate it appears that Neuhaus here equates homosexual orientation with a lack of 'affective maturity'; and affective maturity is undeniably required by the Instruction as a precondition of effective ministry.

These commentators are commonly regarded as articulating a 'conservative' Catholicism, but the view that the Instruction makes homosexual orientation a bar to the priesthood is not confined to theological or religious conservatives. James Martin SJ, an associate editor of *America* magazine, in a PBS *News Hour* discussion with Joespeh Fessio said: '[i]n general, the document is banning people who understand themselves as gay, who understand themselves as having a primarily homosexual orientation, whether or not they can live celibately, and that's that central part that talks about deep-seated homosexual tendencies; at least that's how I read it'.[5] This is the view taken also by Andrew Sullivan, well-known in these islands as a *Sunday Times* journalist, who is gay and a practising Catholic.

A different interpretation has also been voiced. Among its proponents are bishops, cardinals and senior representatives of men's religious orders and congregations. Within a short time of the Instruction's official release, Cardinal Murphy-O'Connor and Bishop William S. Skylstadt, Presidents respectively of the national bishops' conferences of England and Wales and of the United States, issued statements that offered a more benign reading. Cardinal Murphy-O'Connor's statement concludes: 'The Instruction is not saying that men of homosexual orientation are not welcome in the priesthood. Nor should anyone suffer discrimination or prejudice as a result of such orientation.'[6]

The nearest thing to an official Vatican comment occurred in a radio interview given by Cardinal Zenon Grocholewski, Prefect of the Congregation for Catholic

Education, the body from which the document emanated. The Prefect's remarks are helpful in shedding light by way of concrete example upon the meaning of the term 'transient homosexual tendencies', and he makes it clear that a candidate who has acted on such must have ceased to act on them at least three years before ordination as a deacon. His comments include a reiteration of the Instruction's prohibition of involvement in gay culture. But they do not shed light on the meaning of the expression 'deep-seated homosexual tendencies'.[7] On this point, a lengthy article in *l'Osservatore Romano* was taken by some commentators to have quasi-official status. The author is Fr Tony Anatrella, a French psychoanalyst and social psychologist who is a consultor to the Pontifical Councils for the Family and for Health Pastoral Care, and who is said to have been influential in the Instruction's composition. The content and idiom of the article reflect the author's background in psychoanalytic theory. There is little in the way of formal theological argument or canonical jurisprudence, but it is unmistakably a vigorous defence of the view that the Instruction was meant to exclude even chaste homosexuals.[8]

YES OR NO?

What then is one to think? A common-sense approach might be to say that the interpretation proffered by heads of bishops' conferences and other influential Church figures is the one that will prevail. In this connection it is worth bearing in mind that the Instruction itself points out that the call to orders is the personal responsibility of the bishop or major superior. In reaching a judgement on a candidate's suitability the superior or bishop will avail himself of the fruits of a process of discernment in which key roles are played by seminary rectors and others involved in formation.

In trying to make sense of the Instruction, some will doubtless think it enough that the majority of senior churchmen who have commented on it are satisfied that it doesn't exclude every man who has a homosexual orientation.[9] But, of course, any interpretation must be capable of being supported by good reasons, and each of these churchmen has in fact given reasons for his view. Some of them, it must be said, are more convincing than others,[10] and all come up against the fact that in answer to the specific question whether men who have 'deep-seated homosexual tendencies' may be admitted to the seminary and to holy orders, the Instruction clearly answers 'No'.

At this point one might invoke the normal rules of interpretation of documents such as the Instruction, and there are pertinent theological and canonical considerations. No doubt it is relevant that the Church law provides that restrictive legislation must be restrictively interpreted, even if an Instruction of this kind is not a piece of legislation but rather a judgement concerning the concrete requirements of existing law.[11] It is no doubt relevant too that the Pope's approval of the document was general rather than, as the technical expression has it, *in forma specifica*; that is, it does not imply his endorsement of every detail of its contents. Yet there can be no doubt of the Instruction's authority, and what it says cannot be overlooked.

SO?

Are we then to think that this document excludes henceforth from ordination every homosexual man, even if he be chaste and even if in every other respect he is suitable? Someone who argues that it does might add that this way of framing the question introduces an oxymoron, for the Instruction appears to say that a homosexual candidate could never be suitable, since he lacks affective maturity, which is a *sine qua non* of suitability. In fact, the document does not equate affective immaturity and homosexual orientation, even if it comes perilously close to doing so. But does it equate homosexual orientation with 'deep-seated homosexual tendencies'?

This phrase is taken from the *Catechism* and, as in the *Catechism*, it is counterposed to homosexual acts; and it is also counterposed here to 'homosexual tendencies that were only the expression of a transitory problem, for example that of an adolescence not yet superseded'. Since neither homosexual activity nor a homosexual phase necessarily imports homosexual orientation, and since the Instruction doesn't use this last expression, it is easy to see how someone might conclude that homosexual orientation is what is meant by 'deep-seated homosexual tendencies'.

Consider what it says of people with deep-seated homosexual tendencies: 'Such persons, in fact, find themselves in a situation that gravely hinders them from relating correctly to men and women.' Assuming that 'correctly' means something like 'maturely as well as morally properly', the Instruction can hardly wish to say that no homosexual person is capable of right relationship with other men and women. It follows that a simple equation of the terms homosexual orientation and deep-seated homosexual tendencies is not intended. And if that is so it is a mistake to read the document as excluding all homosexual men from the priesthood.

The essential rightness of this view is confirmed, I believe, when one looks at two of the Instruction's cited sources, the *Catechism* and a 1986 *Declaration on Certain Questions Concerning Sexual Ethics*.[12] Both of these insist on the wrongness of homosexual acts, and neither countenances what might nowadays be called a homosexual lifestyle. However, neither is it dogmatic about the nature and genesis of homosexual orientation, and each makes it clear that Catholic teaching requires respect in one's dealings with everyone, homosexual no less than heterosexual. At the conclusion of its brief treatment the *Catechism* states: 'Homosexual persons are called to chastity. By the virtues of self-mastery that teach them inner freedom, at times by the support of disinterested friendship, by prayer and sacramental grace, they can and should gradually and resolutely approach Christian perfection.'[13] This can hardly have envisaged homosexual people as inherently and permanently unable to relate 'correctly' to other women and men.

What I am suggesting is that a hard-line interpretation of the Instruction is not warranted either by its own argument or by the tradition out of which it comes. This must, however, appear a meagre finding by the side of other concerns, including the wider issue of Catholic teaching about homosexuality and, in particular, the idea that a homosexual orientation is *per se* a 'disorder'. And, of course, there remain questions about the theology and practice of priesthood in today's Church.

The Instruction echoes the *Catechism* in speaking of the 'respect and sensitivity' due to homosexual people and in its insistence that 'every sign of unjust discrimination in their regard should be avoided'. However, one may surmise that no amount of explanation in terms of the meaning of the scholastic expression *deordinatio* will allay the fear or soothe the hurt of the homosexual person – or his or her family or friends – who understands the word 'disorder' in any of its normal English usages. And how could anyone think that a reference to 'the current situation' (see the statement of the Instruction's aim above) would not be read as linking homosexuality with child sexual abuse, a linkage which is both erroneous and offensive?

It remains the case that this Instruction is normative for policy in the years ahead and the question of its proper interpretation cannot be sidestepped, not least so that suitable candidates are not deterred from coming forward for ordination. The sensus embodied in the responses of those principally charged with its implementation is encouraging. It can only be hoped that the ekklesia will benefit from the reflection and debate which it has provoked.

NOTES

1   Instruction Concerning the Criteria for the Discernment of Vocations with regard to Persons with Homosexual Tendencies in view of their Admission to the Seminary and to Holy Orders. Congregation for Catholic Education, 4 November 2005. The translation used here is to be found on the Vatican website.
2   Washington Post, 24 November 2005.
3   Father Neuhaus died on 8 January 2009.
4   http://www.firstthings.com/onthesquare/?p=92
5   http://www.pbs.org/newshour/bb/religion/july-dec05/gays_11-29.html
6   The Tablet, 3 December 2005. The double negative in the cardinal's first sentence is indicative of the difficulty involved in reading the Instruction as importing anything even minimally positive about homosexual orientation.
7   See R. Mickens, 'Ambiguous Tendencies', The Tablet, 3 December 2005 (text available via Tablet website). On 31 October 2008 the Congregation for Catholic Education published a document entitled 'Guidelines for the Use of Psychology in the Admission and Formation of Candidates for the Priesthood'. The guidelines concern all candidates for the priesthood and contains little or nothing that is unfamiliar in existing practice, but its reiteration of the phrase 'deep-seated homosexual tendencies' has proved as controversial as did that phrase's appearance in the Instruction discussed here. The Prefect's remarks at the launch of the Guidelines, as reported, shed no further light on the meaning of the phrase: see for example 'Vatican Backs Psychological Screening of Seminarians', The Catholic Herald, 7 November 2008; 'Church in the World', The Tablet, 8 November 2008. The guidelines' contents don't affect the argument offered in the present chapter. An English version of the text is at www.vatican.va/roman_curia/congregations/ccatheduc/documents/rc_con_ccatheduc_doc_20080628_orientamenti_en.html

8   *L'Osservatore Romano*, 29 November 2005.
9   Robert Mickens in *The Tablet*, 31 December 2005 cites a canon lawyer who asked not to be named: 'Bishops make the decisions, not some consultor to a couple of councils.'
10 An article by Timothy Radcliffe OP is especially persuasive: see *The Tablet*, 26 November 2005.
11 *See Code of Canon Law*, canons 18 and 34.
12 www.vatican.va/roman_curia/congregations/cfaith/documents/ rc_con_cfaith_doc_19751229_persona-humana_en.html
13 Par. 2359.

3.
Four Half-Truths and a Lie

Commentary on Pope Benedict's visits to the US, Australia and France has reminded us that it seems to have become impossible to refer to a bishop or theologian, or even a plain believer, without designating him or her conservative or liberal. One could rail against this but railing would alas be in vain, for it looks as if the classification is here to stay. As with the use of the word 'church' when what is meant is church authority, the best that can be hoped for is that the reader, viewer or listener will retain some sense of the terminology's inadequacy, and that he or she will remember that it may sometimes point to a half-truth – or a lie.

READING THE LABEL
In the Catholic church what the label usually means is that its recipient is for or against the following: artificial contraception, divorce, married priests, women priests, legal recognition of homosexual unions (whether as marriage or otherwise) and ecumenism (especially intercommunion). Opinion on contraception, homosexual relationships and divorce is often an element in a more general view of Catholic sexual ethics. Sometimes the liberalisation of church teaching on abortion or on the legalisation of abortion in the civil law is also a marker as, less often perhaps, is euthanasia.

Some comment takes these to belong to 'the Gospel message', and there is rarely any other criterion, though latterly there has been some advertence to Catholic teaching on social justice, as when Pope John Paul II is said to have been 'theologically' conservative while liberal or progressive on human rights. ('Progressive', by the way, is usually an indication of positive regard, which is by no means always true of 'liberal'.) Of course, differences of viewpoint upon the items just listed may be related to differing understandings of the church and of other fundamental matters of the Christian faith. However, at the level of media treatment and of public discussion, these deeper matters don't often get attention.

There is, of course, something to the designations 'conservative' and 'liberal' and their application in this context. In the Catholic Church, there is support for as well as opposition to the items listed, and the position taken on any one item is often – though not always – an index of one's position on the others. And someone who doesn't want change in existing teaching or discipline is appropriately enough called conservative, even if matters are less clear about the use of the terms liberal and progressive. No great harm is done, one supposes, when Cardinal A or theologian B is called liberal or conservative, apart perhaps from annoying those who would like to be thought to belong to the other group.

RISKS

Yet the tendency to classify in this fashion carries risks, not least the risk of laziness in analysing the state of the church and its faith today. This problem is compounded when, for example, liberal stances are identified with fidelity to 'the vision of Vatican II', or conservatism with resistance to the Council's programme. It should go without saying that not every liberal-minded Catholic is in thrall to a godless secularism, nor is every conservative a theocrat; nor – US politics notwithstanding – are the religious or theological leanings signified by the labels a sure guide to a wearer's secular politics.

It is sloppy to invoke the vision of Vatican II as if such a vision can be conjured pristinely out of its context and without regard to what has happened in the church and in the world during the past forty years. There are indeed some characteristic conciliar themes, including that of the vocation of each of the baptised, the centrality of liturgy and especially of the Eucharist, the pursuit of the unity of Christian churches, the importance of conversation with world religions, openness to the world, and the quest for justice and peace. Each of these remains important. A programme for the church, global or local, that made little of any of them would not be faithful to the Council.

CHANGES
These themes and what the Council made of them do not exhaust the implications of the Gospel or the requirements of evangelisation now. For the world has meanwhile changed. The Council didn't know of globalisation or of multiculturalism; of the European Union; of the failure of soviet communism and the emergence of the United States as sole superpower; of the possibilities of information and biomedical technologies; of AIDS and of ecological damage; of international terrorism and new possibilities of mass destruction; of all that is meant by the rise of the religious right. One can see why some of the Council's utterances might now seem too optimistic, even as one wants to hold on to its hopes.

The church also has changed. How could the Council Fathers have foreseen the dimensions of its growth in Africa, for example, or of its decline in western Europe? Many hoped for an internationalisation of the Roman curia, but who in 1965 could have foreseen a Polish and a German pope? When the vocation of the baptised was emphasised, and the priesthood of the laity and the value of lay apostolate, who saw the urgency these themes would acquire in large areas of the church, as vocations to the ordained priesthood and to the religious life declined? Who realised that a world-wide movement for the recognition of women's rights would lead to radical questioning of Catholic attitudes and practices? Who foresaw our time's interest in spirituality? And did anyone foresee (see?) the extent of the abuse of children by priests, bishops, brothers and nuns?

Many changes are for the better, of course, but the point just now is that, good or bad, they make our world different from that in which the Second Vatican Council took place. The changing times have brought new questions and new challenges for Gospel proclamation and witness. Some questions faced by the Council are still with us, some even more urgently now than then. However, now they may appear in a different light, and solutions pointed to at the Council and in its aftermath may no longer avail. The doctrine of the 'just war', for example, is part of Christian moral heritage, but what is its bearing on the use of weapons of mass destruction? Religious freedom was affirmed unambiguously in *Dignitatis humanae*, but how does it stand in the face of religious fundamentalism? What is the connection now between liturgy and life, life and liturgy, and what is Christian spirituality? How is the saving message of Jesus to be preached to all peoples now?

RESPONSES

The new situation is not adequately met by way of tired standard 'conservative' or 'liberal' reaction, and will certainly not be met if the kind of polarisation which afflicts much Catholic thought and action today is allowed to settle into rigidity and hardness of heart. Peter Steinfels makes an important observation in this regard:

Liberals and conservatives raise the same fears, make the same complaints, offer the same arguments, as they did twenty years ago. Has the world stood still, one wonders, since the Second Vatican Council? Can nothing be concluded from more than three decades of post-conciliar experience? Wouldn't it be a remarkable coincidence if liberals were proven right about absolutely everything, and conservatives wrong – or vice versa?[1]

These are not merely trite points, and they are valid not only for the US church. It is a depressing fact that even serious discussion often gives an impression of *parti pris*, and instead of reasoned argument there is only a rehearsal of positions that make no attempt to engage with each other. Some will maintain that this is a result of policies that have discouraged and even penalised theological exploration. Others will contend that the repetition of traditional or official positions is precisely what is called for when those positions are settled doctrine and when the questions are no more than the modish questions of an unsettled time.

Hence a liberal-minded Catholic might claim that the church's *magisterium* has been ignoring the questions, and so the questions must be repeated. A conservative-type rejoinder might be that in matters of definitively taught doctrine and discipline no questions can be permitted. Each of these responses points to a truth, but that doesn't mean that either is the end of the story. *Magisterium* has in fact been exercised in response to the concerns usually called liberal, and there has been a reiteration of teaching central in Catholic tradition, including teaching that is unchangeable.

However, the question of what is or is not changeable is itself sometimes controversial, and parties to that debate don't always display the patience that the question requires. Neither is it satisfactory when an issue is settled as it were by decree. And there is potential for injustice, as was said earlier, when liberal or conservative tags are taken to point to more basic loyalties. It is simply not true that only the liberal-minded have the spirit of Vatican II or that conservative views are the only views compatible with fidelity to the Gospel of Jesus Christ.

'I AM FOR RAHNER'. 'I AM FOR VON BALTHASAR'. 'I AM FOR BENEDICT XVI'[2]

Or Augustine or Aquinas or Pope John XXIII. But Aquinas was indebted to Augustine, and Pope Benedict would no doubt acknowledge a debt to both – and to Rahner and von Balthasar and the Pope of the Council. All these are among the most prominent of Christians; each differs in background, history, make-up; but all followed the way of the Lord Jesus and in each of them faith sought and seeks understanding, which is the business of Christian theology.

In the church there will always be differences in theological approach and in styles of leadership, and these will sometimes be marked and perhaps strongly expressed. Paul's reproof to quarrelling Corinthians will sometimes need to be recalled. It is one thing when principle divides, and it sometimes must, but it is lamentable when a mere partisanship distorts vision and breeds bitterness among people who count themselves Christian. This is not just a matter of individual impiety for, as John T. Noonan has put it, in the intellectual climate we inhabit, it is dangerous for the church when theological warfare breaks out.[3]

A WAY AHEAD?

Peter Steinfels in the passage quoted goes on to say: 'The time has come for analyses and recommendations that freely cross liberal–conservative party lines – and that also seek insight in the experiences of other religious groups.'[4]

He is thinking primarily of pastoral measures and of developments in discipline and practice; but, of course, the practical presupposes a theory, a theology (or theologies) responsive to the needs of our times and of every place in which the Gospel is preached. What are the prospects?

Some hope that Pope Benedict's papacy has inaugurated a new and more positive phase in the life of Catholicism, a gentler time in which *listening* – on the part of leaders and led, theology and magisterium, local church and the centre of universal government – will have a greater role. Indeed the Pope has himself already emphasised the importance of listening, and not just to the experience of Roman Catholic Christians. Listening doesn't come easy to people who have learned to tune out the voice of the other on suspicion of difference of viewpoint or to dismiss the other's question (or reply) on the basis of a tag. Yet listening is a prerequisite for understanding, at this point in the life of the church perhaps more than ever – not to say for the love to which Christians are called and profess.

Inevitably one's notion of other pre-requisites will reflect one's own experience, and mine, for almost all of the time since the Council, has been of the world of Catholic moral theology. The turbulence of that world during that time is well documented and doesn't need recounting here. Suffice it to say that practitioners of moral theology, conservative and liberal, are among those hoping for a gentler time, and not just for the sake of personal equilibrium. For our age is putting ceaseless pressure on the resources of the Catholic moral tradition, as our world changes with unprecedented speed. Unresolved questions, of the kind that have divided conservative and liberal, include moral issues that have perplexed faithful Catholics for some time.

I should like to make only one main point about this, in the shape of a two-fold observation. This is that the questions which modern moral theology canvasses – questions of human dignity and equality, human rights, gender and sexuality, politics, the ethics of globalisation and of technological advance – are not invented by the morally wayward but are born in unfolding human experience. Their complexity is such that it cannot but be that some of them provoke a diversity of response, including among Catholics.

This is so even though we have inherited a moral tradition that points unequivocally to the enduring and absolute claims of such values as that of life and of love, of justice and of peace. For the concrete requirements of these claims are not always obvious and what was concretely said at an earlier time may need to be reviewed in changed circumstances. Again one need only think of the doctrine of the just war and the US bishops' account of this in their pastoral letter *The Challenge of Peace*,[5] where they distinguish between unchangeable principle (in this case that it is always wrong directly to take innocent life) and its 'prudential application' in the then current circumstances. The difficulty of achieving absolute clarity in applying general principle to particular situations was remarked by Aquinas,[6] and that kind of difficulty has not gone away.

It is therefore unhelpful, in reference to problems some Catholics have with particular items of the moral tradition, to speak of *à la carte* Catholicism, as though what is in question always is self-indulgent choice according to current middle-class taste.[7] More crass still is the response that the church is a club and that if you join it you should keep the club's rules. Leaving aside the differences between the moral order and the rules of a club, consider only the account of the nature of the church that the Council gave in *Lumen gentium*. The first two chapters are entitled respectively 'The Mystery of the Church' and 'The People of God', and the first explores the mystery through (among other images) the Pauline idea of the mystical body of Christ. A *club*?

John T. Noonan in the same article has some advice in relation to current conflict in the church: 'Don't enlarge differences. Don't turn differences into doctrinal defaults. Keep the harmony. Remember that a symphony comes from many distinct instruments, each played in its own way. Benedict XVI will conduct.'[8] The advice applies to everyone in the church. The idealism in the metaphor need not distract from the practical wisdom. And we might remember Lumen gentium.

NOTES

1   Peter Steinfels, A People Adrift: The Crisis in the Roman Catholic Church in America, New York: Simon and Schuster 2003, reissued 2004 with a new Afterword and Agenda, p. 10.
2   See 1 Corinthians 1:10ff.
3   John T. Noonan, 'Mending the Harmony of the Church', The Furrow, September 2005, p. 457. Noonan's diagnosis of the western intellectual climate vis-à-vis religion, and especially Christianity, is a familiar one. Some may wonder whether it is unduly negative; at the least, the religions need to try to understand and evaluate the hostility, and not just to condemn it. Of course, Noonan is right about the readiness of enemies to exploit the church's ruptures; and in any case, importantly, he adds: '... not only are ruptures exploited in this hostile intellectual environment. Ruptures are an internal blow. They wound what should be a single interacting organism' (ibid.).
4   Steinfels, loc. cit.
5   Washington, 1983.
6   Summa Theologiae 1a 2ae, 94, 4.
7   The conceit is, of course, witty, as is that of cafeteria Catholic, a nod perhaps to the fact that the questions don't all come from the well-heeled.
8   Ibid. Judge Noonan, author of several important books in the history of moral theology, is a member of the Committee of the Catholic Common Ground Initiative, founded by the late Cardinal Bernardin to promote constructive discussion between liberal and conservative elements in the US church. He is regarded as a conservative, a fact which makes his valuable article – taken from the Initiative's June 2005 Report – the more interesting. Lest his advice seem a touch rhapsodic it should be said that the article includes some hard analysis of the canon law of marriage, and some plainly expressed views about moral magisterium.

4.
Child Sexual Abuse:
Some Rules for the Debate

'Peter Saunders is a man torn between loyalty to the Church and loyalty to victims of clerical abuse.' So begins an article in a recent issue of *The Tablet*. Peter Saunders has good reason to wish to be loyal to victims of sexual abuse by clerics and religious, for he himself is a survivor. It should go without saying that the sense of being torn must be at its most acute in someone who has been abused and in whom religious faith and church allegiance have yet persisted. The description of his dilemma will strike a chord even in people who have not been abused but who have entered, so far as this is possible, into the sufferings of the abused, and who wish only both that justice is fully done and that the Catholic Church comes through the current controversy. I mean, of course, people for whom faith and church allegiance are important, those people who have been shocked, angered, thrown into a profound dismay by the ceaseless spate of revelations of harm and of betrayal of trust, but who are nevertheless held by their religious convictions and loyalties and who want, desperately, a truthful and just end to the present distress.

It is difficult to live with the tension generated by these loyalties and it is difficult sometimes to avoid reacting: against the church leader who, despite everything, still seems more interested in defending church institutions than in acknowledging fault and making reparation; against the journalist who takes liberties with the facts, spins a story or a headline, questions the bona fides of those who are manifestly trying to deal with the situation in the best way they can; sometimes even against a survivor who seems implacable, intent only on a revenge which is blind in its object and in its methods.

There is no comparing, it is rightly said, the sufferings of victims and the pain of those who must now answer for the failures of the 'institutional' Church. Probably only someone who has been abused can empathise adequately with the suffering of the abused. Particularly if one is a religious or cleric, one needs to be constantly on guard lest one's responses are merely reactionary. Yet one sometimes feels for the church representative whose honest effort to right past wrongs is met only with incredulity and derision.

Perhaps we are still at a stage in the process of disclosure/reparation when it is impossible to think straight concerning what has been uncovered about the misdoings of Catholic clergy and religious, and about the ineptitude and sometimes dishonesty with which complaints have been met. Some people fear that we shall never emerge from it. However, attempts to think straight and to act justly and with compassion, whether in reference to complainants or to those against whom the complaints are being made, are not helped by the kind of polarisation which constantly threatens.

POLARISATION

It is depressing to be a party to conversations in which all media people are assumed to be interested only in getting at 'us' and in circulation or audience figures. Some are; some aren't. Of course, it is depressing too to meet evidence of suspicion and hostility towards all clergy and religious on the basis of the conduct of some. These are extremes. Probably most people still are somewhere in the middle, pulled now this way, now that – sharing, if they are Catholics, in the kind of dilemma felt by Peter Saunders.

How do attitudes become polarised? There are, I suppose, people who start off polarised, so to speak – people who are determined to hold to their side of the story regardless of what is said by those on the other side. This can only beget an equal and opposite reaction, and positions on both sides are hardened, perhaps irremediably. But there is another way in which polarisation may occur: that is, when someone or some group come to believe that they are not being heard, when they feel that no matter what they say, whatever the truth, falsehood and injustice are what will prevail.

Polarisation precludes reconciliation – one should perhaps say, precludes truth, the only sure basis for healing and for a prospectful resolution of all of the problems that attend child sexual abuse. There are people who, wholly understandably, will never be reconciled to the horrific contradictions involved in the abuse of children by men and women in whom, in virtue of their religious authority, absolute trust was placed. It is impossible to guess how many Catholics, themselves victims/survivors or not, will walk no more in the faith in which they were raised.

That, obviously, is a problem for the Catholic Church and its leadership, and just now it is not at all obvious how it might be met. However, this is only part of the problem facing the wider Irish community, for even were the 'Catholic' problem to achieve some sort of resolution, there is still the fact that abuse by religious personnel accounts for under 5 per cent of the extent of the problem in Ireland.[1] Polarisation always threatens resolution, but a polarisation which is untrue to the facts must make resolution impossible.

I said earlier that it may be that we are still at a stage in the process of disclosure/reparation when it is impossible to think straight; if that is so, the hope for a constructive public debate upon the issues is for the moment remote.

It may also be that for various reasons a public working-through of the specifically Catholic Church dimension of the problematic is necessary before the wider problem can even be addressed. In terms of the purging of the Church, it is imperative that no short-circuiting of this process is attempted. However, it is well to keep in mind that the wider problem will not be addressed so long as we are locked into the Church context. And even the Church dimension cannot adequately be addressed if a polarisation of viewpoint is allowed to set the terms of debate.

RESOLUTION? 'RULES FOR THE DEBATE'

More than a quarter of a century ago, at an especially low moment in the abortion debate in the US, the late Richard McCormick SJ commented upon the destructive polarisation that had come to mark the debate. He acknowledged the difficulty in breaking through to a space in which disciplined and constructive argument might take place, but he ventured a suggestion. 'Many of us have become bone weary of this discussion. But to yield to such fatigue would be to run from a problem, not wrestle with it. If stay we ought and must, then it may be of help to propose a set of "rules for conversation", the observance of which could nudge us towards more communicative conversation.'[2] He formulated a set of nine such 'rules', some of which might be instructive for us.

Discussion about child sexual abuse is not, of course, a debate in the sense that one might have a debate about abortion legislation. No one, for example, wants to say that child sexual abuse is defensible, no one doubts that those who perpetrate it must be brought to book and no one (I hope) seriously doubts that those who have or have had a position of responsibility in relation either to abusers or to the abused must be called to account. What is and will be in debate is the detail, or some of it:

the procedures for dealing with complaints, the remedies available to complainants, the best way to deal with the convicted, the nature and degree of accountability of those in authority, the adequacy of responses to date – above all, the measures to be taken to ensure that children are protected for the future.

So there is need for debate. Even if calm debate is not yet possible or at present even foreseeable, some of McCormick's 'rules', *mutatis mutandis*, could help in an Irish public debate about child sexual abuse. For example, he calls on protagonists to attempt to identify areas of agreement, to represent the opposing position accurately and fairly, and to try to identify the core issues at stake. These seem obvious, bland even, and yet only with difficulty are they implemented in practice. McCormick explains why the first can be troublesome: 'Where issues are urgent and disputants have enormous personal stakes and investments, there is a tendency to draw sharp lines very quickly and begin the shootout.'[3] The same dynamic will militate against the implementation of the second and third rules.

Two other rules, adapted, could improve our debate and the prospects of a good outcome: as expressed by McCormick they are *Avoid the use of slogans* and *Distinguish the pairs right–wrong, good–bad.* Elaborating on the first he writes: 'Slogans are the weapons of the crusader, one who sees his role as warfare, generally against those sharply defined as "the enemy"'. Fighting for good causes clearly has its place, as do slogans, but slogans are not very enlightening conversational tools, simply because they bypass and effectively subvert the process of communication'.[4] Sloganising, or something like it, occurs when, for example, media coverage of child sexual abuse in the Catholic Church is said to be motivated by anticlericalism, hostility to religion or concern for sales or figures. It occurs also when all church authorities are portrayed as interested solely in the preservation of the institution. It occurs when – one hopes now rarely – complainants are dismissed as cranks, neurotics, troublemakers. And it occurs when abusers are scapegoated or demonised.

RIGHT AND WRONG; GOOD AND BAD

The meaning of the second rule, *Distinguish the pairs right–wrong, good–bad*, may not be immediately clear from this formulation. It refers to the fact that one might perform a wrong action without being to blame, or fully to blame; and so one ought not, on that basis, be judged a bad person. By the same token, one might perform a good action without, by that fact, establishing oneself as 'good'. The reason for this is that a moral evaluation takes into account not only what I do, but what I *understand and mean* by what I do, as well as the *circumstances* which may, as the saying goes, alter cases.

I could do something that is on the face of it 'right' (helping someone in need) for the wrong reason or with a wrong attitude (out of a desire to impress, patronisingly, motivated solely by guilt); and the moral value of what I have done is accordingly impaired. It is also the case that someone who has done evil things, who was perhaps an evil person, may repent their wrongdoing and try to live a good life again. So from the fact that someone has *acted wrongly*, it doesn't follow that she or he is a *bad person*; and since the outsider normally doesn't know what goes on in the heart of another, or what the full circumstances are, it behoves us not to judge.[5] This doesn't detract a whit from our entitlement to be appalled at wrongdoing and to condemn it in the strongest terms. It does, however, affect the question of how we ought to deal with the wrongdoer.

When a particularly horrific evil is perpetrated, it is difficult to keep the distinction here in question in mind. We saw this not long ago in public reaction to the death of Myra Hindley: there were people who could not be persuaded that someone who caused so much evil might have repented, let alone that a psychopathology might have diminished her culpability in the first place. Similar reactions follow disclosure of the more shocking instances of child sexual abuse. Some people are impatient with suggestions that those who abuse children often do so because they themselves have been abused; and they are dismissive of suggestions that the convicted should be given an opportunity for rehabilitation. Some are unable to accept that a child abuser might repent and change his or her ways.

The distinction alluded to by McCormick cannot be dismissed as yet another instance of verbal gymnastics of a sort sometimes ascribed by their critics to ethicians. It is recognised by the law, which takes an accused's 'mind' or inner psychological state into account before giving judgement as to guilt and in deciding on an appropriate penalty. In any case, it is familiar in everyday less dramatic experience, for we find ourselves recognising that someone who does something wrong 'couldn't be blamed', for he or she 'couldn't help it', either because of ignorance, mistake or because driven by fear, or by some compulsion outside of conscious control. Neither is it right to dismiss the possibility of someone's repenting their wrongdoing and starting again on the path of good living. This too is a matter of common human experience, the experience of each one of us in our own case. To deny this possibility is at odds directly with the Judeo-Christian religious tradition, which affirms the constancy of God's forgiving love and the permanence of God's invitation to repentance.

It is understandable when those who have suffered abuse, whose suffering has perhaps been aggravated by attempts to evade responsibility and to cover up, are unable to acknowledge such distinctions and possibilities – which makes it all the more moving and humbling when individuals display the kind of understanding and compassion which recognition of them calls for. It is a different matter when outsiders – and I'm thinking here especially of some (repeat, *some*) media commentary – depict attempts to draw attention to these dimensions as attempts at institutional self-exculpation or, worse, as seeking to minimise the enormity of abusers' crimes.

THREE MORE RULES

The foregoing was suggested by McCormick's 'rules for conversation', adapted to fit the subject matter and the circumstances in which the Irish debate on child sexual abuse is taking place and will develop. To the selection from McCormick's list here presented I think we might add three further proposals.

The first is that all parties should respect each other's bona fides. I grant that this is difficult, if not impossible in some cases. How can you accept the bona fides of a church or other official if you even suspect that that official's concern is not with your problem but with protecting the institutions of which he or she is representative and custodian? One fears lest there are such still. How can church people respect the bona fides of a media person or other commentator who is determined to have the last ounce of the last pound of flesh, regardless of accuracy, regardless of the claims of fairness. One fears that there are such still. The bona fides of complainants must always be respected, but that cannot mean ignoring the fact that some accusations are false.

The second rule is that there must be 'patient attention to the facts' – the phrase, I think, is Iris Murdoch's. What are the facts about the incidence of child abuse among the clergy? Do we know any facts about the putative connection between the present discipline of celibacy and child sexual abuse? (It cannot be right to refuse to explore the possibility.) Are there different kinds of offenders? What are the facts about the possibilities for rehabilitating some kinds? What is the incidence of re-offending? What are the facts about this or that particular person who has been convicted and who has paid the penalty laid down by law? Discussion so far has not always been marked by patient attention to the facts.

The third rule is one specific to the debate about child abuse by Catholic clerics and religious. It might at first sight look like the kind of nicety that could trouble only someone who had nothing pressing to think about. Yet I believe that, from the Church's point of view, it is of profound importance in this as in so many other matters. It is that the word 'Church' should not be used when what is meant is church leaders or members of the clergy or religious communities. The Second Vatican Council went to pains to repudiate the notion that 'Church' is identified with office-holders and those ordained or consecrated to special roles or states. That hasn't put an end to the practice – including among church leaders and officials themselves – of speaking as though it is.

This is not, I'm afraid, a piece of harmless carelessness. For a start it may distort the perception of the dilemma expressed by Peter Saunders. Loyalty to 'the Church' is loyalty to the *whole community* called Church. Normally this calls for loyalty to the leadership, but, of course, victims who are Catholic are also of the Church, as are their families and friends, and as are the people envisaged here as sharing, even if differently, in the kind of dilemma in which Peter Saunders finds himself. Loyalty to the Church may require stringent criticism of leadership and it will certainly require resistance to any attempt to evade responsibility in the matter of child sexual abuse.

A second unfortunate consequence of the identification of the Church with its leaders or officials is that these latter may well come to make the identification, even if only unconsciously. And any propensity to envisage the situation as one of 'them' and 'us' risks being intensified accordingly. This appears to have happened in some dioceses in the US where, astonishingly, some priests were reported as regarding the laity who became involved in the controversy as engaged in some sort of power bid. It can only be hoped that such a bizarre misjudgement is not made here.

Third – again as with other matters – when the Church is conceived only in terms of hierarchical leaders and officials, it is all too easy for other members to ignore their own responsibilities. Those in official positions have, of course, first responsibility both as to what went wrong and as to how it may be righted. However – especially as to how wrong may now be righted – we all share responsibility, whatever the ways in any given situation this responsibility is to be exercised.

It is not, I hope, unrealistic to look forward to a time when the problem of child sexual abuse in Ireland can be addressed calmly but with maximum effectiveness. As far as the Catholic Church is concerned, in Ireland as elsewhere, it has generated a massive problem of credibility and yet, amazingly, there is a store of good will which may sustain those charged with the task of trying to bring some healing. One hopes, of course, that no one in authority in the Church is in any doubt now as to the gravity of the problem, in itself and as, literally, a scandal; and one hopes that the good will is not misinterpreted or squandered. For the Church debate and for the wider debate that is still to come, perhaps some 'rules' such as those here suggested might not come amiss.

NOTES

1   SAVI Report, commissioned by the Dublin Rape Crisis Centre.
2   Richard McCormick, *How Brave a New World?*, London: SCM, 1981, Chapter 9, 'Rules for Abortion Debate', pp. 176–187. This first appeared in *America* 139 (1978), pp. 26–30.
3   Ibid., p. 177.
4   Op. cit., p. 178.
5   The case is different with the law, for a court must judge guilt or innocence *before the law*, and it will have rules of evidence and other procedures which try to ensure that this is done as fairly as possible.

5.
Justice Tempered by Love[1]

A commonplace of commentary following the death of John Paul II was that though conservative on sexual morality he was progressive in his social teaching. Pope Benedict was expected to be no less conservative on sexual morality, but commentators evinced surprise at his positive appraisal of eros in *Deus caritas est*, even as they scanned the second part of the encyclical for evidence of a retrenchment on some of the positions on social justice which his predecessor had taken.

There is some truth in such generalisations and, on the whole, they are probably harmless. However, they may mask preconceptions of a kind that can distort the Christian gospel. It is still possible to meet the view that morality is about sexuality and about nothing much else, and it is still possible to meet the view that 'social' teaching isn't really about morality at all. A related notion is that whereas sexual ethics are at the core of Christian moral doctrine, teaching about social justice is peripheral, and not at all to be taken as seriously. This latter becomes entangled sometimes with another question, that of the scope and binding character of official Catholic teaching. Students of Church–State relations in the Ireland of the 1950s may recall an attempt to discredit the Catholic bishops' approach to Dr Noel Browne's Mother and Child scheme by saying that it was 'only' social teaching and, therefore, not binding on the consciences of politicians or people. Lest it be thought that this distinction was peculiar to a benighted Ireland half a century ago, a glance at the debate surrounding the US bishops' pastoral *Economic*

Justice for All (1983) will indicate its persistence in a very different time and place.

There are reasons for these misconceptions and confusions, odd as they now appear, and we shall be touching on some of them later. However, it may as well be noted at the outset that there is no Christian warrant for minimising the place of social responsibilities, the 'social vocation', the mutual responsibilities of community and members, and the responsibilities also *vis-à-vis* the lesser communities of which we are each also a part. A spirituality which would have members withdraw from engagement with the challenges of living in today's world is one form of Christian spirituality but it is not the only form, nor by itself could it suffice as witness to the riches of the Gospel message.

'THE SPIRIT OF THE LORD'

One has only to remember the beginning of Jesus' public ministry as this is told by Luke: he reads in the synagogue a prophecy of Isaiah, which speaks of an anointing by the Spirit of the Lord that confers a mission to bring good news to the poor, proclaim release to the captive, sight to the blind and freedom from oppression; and he tells them that on this day that prophecy is being fulfilled. There is indeed a place for contemplation even – indeed especially – for one who is living a life of active apostolate in the world, and Jesus himself provides an example in this regard. However, an emphasis on the need for contemplation should not seek to devalue commitment to the Church's work of justice and of peace.

The fact remains that for a variety of reasons this dimension of gospel witness was not always or sufficiently honoured, though we needn't here take time over what it is anachronistic to bewail. For reasons to do with the kind of books they were – textbooks for training future priests for the work of the confessional – the manuals of moral theology in use from the beginning of the seventeenth century to the middle of the twentieth dealt with questions of justice largely in terms of individual and interpersonal justice, and matters of 'distributive' and 'legal' justice, as social justice was called, were treated only briefly if at all. Even after social justice became a theme of papal teaching it was some time before it came to be regarded as a standard item in Catholic moral theology.

A standard item it is now though, and the scope of the term has broadened to include not just the ethics of the interrelationships of individual and society but also the interrelationships of individual and society with the *societies* of which the larger society is constituted – marriage, family, the world of work and so on. Indeed, as a glance at the *Compendium of the Social Doctrine of the Church*[2] shows, Catholic social teaching is now concerned with nothing less than the entire canvas of human social relationships.

OF NEW THINGS

The corpus to which the name 'social teaching' is given has its origin in an encyclical of Leo XIII, *Rerum novarum*, published in 1891, and the term is associated in a special way with the magisterium of the popes since then. However, it is worth noting that vital contributions have been made also by the Second Vatican Council, by a Synod of the world's bishops in 1971, by local and regional episcopal teaching bodies and by the permanent secretariat of the Pontifical Council for Justice and Peace, which is responsible for the *Compendium*. Nor should it be forgotten that Catholic social thought is continually enriched by the witness of praxis throughout the world.[3]

That a distinctive social doctrine began to evolve during the papacy of Leo XIII was a consequence of great societal change in Europe during the nineteenth century, and at the centre of this change was what we now call the Industrial Revolution. For this bespoke new social realities and unprecedented social problems, as crowds of men, women and children came to live and work in towns and cities, and as the question of the value and circumstances of their labour as well as the necessities of their livelihood came into view against a background of capitalist economics. A second key factor was the rise of the nation states and of liberal democratic forms of government. How was government to promote social order in the changed situation, how to ensure just distribution of property and the new wealth, how to safeguard and enhance the conditions for a true human fulfillment for all people of every class? And – a different type of question but plainly also critical – how to ensure participation in the new political systems so that peoples could truly govern themselves?

It is usual to observe that a constructive Catholic answer to these and related questions was late in coming, and that is true if we are thinking only of the emergence with Leo XIII of a papal social teaching which began to stand as an official challenge to the way in which employers were treating workers, and to the conditions in which so many were expected to live their lives. However, this is to forget a different kind of witness to Gospel values that long predated the encyclical, the care for the poor and the sick that was the mission of so many orders and congregations of women and men, not to mention the work of lay movements such as Frederic Ozanam's St Vincent de Paul Society.

RIGHTS TALK
It remains true that church leaders had been wary of political ideas associated with the revolutions of the late eighteenth and the nineteenth centuries. In particular, they had been opposed to anything that appeared to savour of 'socialism'. Pope Leo and several of his successors were

at pains to make it clear that there was a right to private property, and indeed that right is still affirmed in Catholic teaching. Limitations as to its exercise, clearly evident in patristic and scholastic thinking, were not in the forefront of Leo's mind, but they are intimated more and more clearly in each of the social encyclicals since his time.

Church leaders had been wary too of the notion of human rights, in part again because of its association with political philosophies and revolutionary movements which targeted religion and church as well as aristocracies. Leo, even if cautiously, overcame the suspicion attendant on 'rights talk', insisting on the entitlement of workers to a just wage, to decent working conditions and to association for the promotion and defence of their rightful interests. With the papacy of John XXIII the church's magisterium was making free use of the concepts and devices of human rights discourse, and this way of thinking and talking about morality is now characteristic of Catholic social thought.

What we have seen in the hundred and twenty or so years since Leo's encyclical then is the incremental development of a body of official Catholic teaching which addresses the life of today's man and woman in today's world. That life and our world are full of complexity, and so the teaching is complex. Yet its essence lies in a few ideas that may be simply enough expressed. For in essence it is only an elaboration of the call of Jesus that we should have love, one for another.

Easier said than done, of course, and it is not always easy to know what love requires. A starting point in Catholic social thought is that each human being is made in the image of God, so that each possesses an intrinsic dignity, and we each possess it equally; and that dignity calls for acknowledgment; and acknowledgement means giving people what is their due, and in the first place what is their due by virtue simply of being human. What *that* is, spelled out, may be found in any modern standard enumeration of human rights, following the first international instrument, the UN Declaration on Human Rights of 1948. The extent to which Catholic social teaching makes the content of these enumerations its own may be seen from a reading of the *Compendium*.

So the demands of the commandment that we should have love, one for another, may be specified in terms of regard for human rights, even if such (or any) specification cannot capture in full the meaning of *agape*. It is plain that these rights have to be protected, promoted and defended; and that, human nature being what it is, there is necessarily a role for law and the institutions of state; and, indeed, that some rights can be assured of implementation only through the mechanisms of government and law.

WHAT IS IT TO BE HUMAN?

However, Catholic social teaching is not confined to an endorsement of the entitlements that have come to be recognised as human rights; nor does it purport to say how every right is concretely to be implemented. What it does is offer a vision of the human in the light of which human rights and responsibilities may be understood. The vision includes transcendence as to human origins, identity and destiny; and it transforms and illuminates, so that, sin notwithstanding, what is created is also seen as graced.

The view of human rights offered by this teaching is not visionary only, and there is much that is concrete and practical – about citizenship, the family, political life, international relations, about the realities of life lived in the *polis* in our time. A controlling idea, put negatively, is that it seeks to avoid the excesses of both an individualistic and a collectivist approach. More positively, there are characteristic emphases, some of them having the force of principles, whose intent is to this effect.

COMMON GOODS

The most basic of these is the teaching's insistence on the importance of having regard to the 'common good'. This expression, and to some extent the idea, has an ancient pedigree in Graeco-Roman philosophy and is found in the writings of the medieval scholastic theologians, notably St Thomas Aquinas. Similar expressions – common welfare, for example, or common weal, or commonwealth – can be found in more modern philosophies, as can alternatives such as public good, public welfare and the like. And, of course, the term has latterly become part of the rhetoric of democratic politics in many countries of the world.[4]

But the notion of a common good, contrasted with individual or personal good, has been understood differently at different times and by different users of the term. Even within Catholic social teaching there are tensions in concept and usage that can be perplexing. Yet it is possible to identify some persistent themes in the teaching and, following the account found in the *Catechism of the Catholic Church*, it is possible to present in systematic form the main lines of a Catholic understanding of the common good.

The core insight is that the human person is a social, relational or community being; and this is not just because we need others for the necessities of survival but because we flourish only in the measure in which the person transcends self in love. The good of every person is found in community with others, and there is a common good – better perhaps, common goods – which are the context and accompaniment of the fulfilment of each.

In a phrase from Vatican II's *Gaudium et spes* which echoes Pope John's *Mater et magistra*, the *Catechism* declares that the common good is 'the sum of those conditions of social life which allow both social groups and their individual members relatively thorough and ready access to their own fulfilment'. This is, of course, a quite general description; one must ask, what are these conditions? The *Catechism* sets them out in summary form in terms of 'three essential elements'. First, there are 'the fundamental and inalienable rights of the human person', among which explicit mention is made of the right to follow conscience. Second, the common good requires 'the social well-being and development of the group itself'; and the civil authority 'should make accessible to each what is needed to lead a truly human life: food, clothing, health, work, education and culture, suitable information, the right to establish a family and so on'. Third, the common good requires peace, 'that is, the stability and security of a just order'.

It was suggested above that one might speak of common goods. This is because, as the *Catechism* puts it, 'each human community possesses a common good which permits it to be recognised as such'. Catholic social teaching in general makes special mention of 'intermediate' communities – those groupings other than the political community of which the person may also be a member. However, 'it is in the political community that its [the common good] most complete realisation is found' and 'it is the role of the state to defend and promote the common good of civil society, its citizens and intermediate bodies'.

There is a further dimension of the common good which has been disclosing itself in our times, the Catechism notes: 'Human interdependence is increasing and gradually spreading throughout the world. The unity of the human family, embracing people who enjoy equal natural dignity, implies a universal common good.' This good requires 'an organisation of the community of nations' that will be able to provide for the different needs of people, including food, hygiene, education, seeking in particular to alleviate the miseries of refugees throughout the world, and assisting migrants and their families.

An insistence on the common good or common goods is clearly a counterbalance to individualism. However, it is important to hold in mind that, as is plain from the foregoing, in Catholic social thought the common good is nevertheless not something *over against* individual freedom; rather is the individual's freedom a part of the common good. Nor is the common good the aggregate of individual goods, or the good of a majority is society. It's instructive to recall that the common good was a theme of writers such as Jacques Maritain who were as opposed to totalitarianisms of the right and left as much as to unbridled individualism.

A second key emphasis in Catholic social teaching is what is somewhat cumbersomely called the universal destination of goods. What it means is put plainly in words from the Second Vatican Council's *Gaudium et spes*: 'God destined the earth and all it contains for all men and all peoples so that all created things would be shared fairly by all mankind under the guidance of justice tempered by charity.' This is, says the *Compendium*, a natural right, innate and antecedent to all positive law, so that, as Paul VI in *Populorum progressio* expressed it: 'All other rights, whatever they are, including property rights and the right of free trade must be subordinated to this norm; they must not hinder it, but must rather expedite its application. It must be considered a serious and urgent social obligation to refer these rights to their original purpose.'

SOLIDARITIES
A third characteristic emphasis is on human solidarity. The term inevitably evokes memories of the Polish trade union led by Lech Walesa, and also of Pope John Paul II

in whose political and social philosophy it had a key role. As used in magisterial teaching, the idea goes back to an early stage in the development of Catholic social thought. It was associated especially with the influential work of the German Jesuit Heinrich Pesch, whose student Oswald von Nell-Breuning was centrally involved in drafting Pius XI's *Quadragesimo anno.*

The term refers in the first place to the factual interdependence of human beings, an interdependence that in our world is found at all levels, and indeed includes the mutual relationships of human and other life that are the concern of ecology. Human beings are inherently social, cannot come to be or to grow apart from in relationships of many and varied kinds. The solidarity thus engendered needs to be acknowledged and respected: there needs to be a *sense* of our solidarity with humankind and with the rest of creation, which will include a sense of our *responsibility* for each other and for our world.

The *Compendium* puts the moral challenge in clear terms: 'In the presence of the phenomenon of interdependence and its constant expansion ... there persist in every part of the world stark inequalities between developed and developing countries, inequalities stoked also by various forms of exploitation, oppression and corruption that have a negative influence on the internal and international life of many States. The acceleration of interdependence between persons and peoples needs to be accompanied by equally intense efforts on the ethical–social plane, in order to avoid the dangerous consequences of perpetrating injustice on a global scale.' A commitment to solidarity 'translates into the willingness to give oneself for the good of one's neighbour, beyond any individual or particular interest'.

SUBSIDIARITIES

A fourth emphasis is one that has achieved currency even in secular social thought, that known as the principle of subsidiarity. *Subsidium* is a Latin word for help or support. At one level, the principle refers to the fact that individuals and social groups require for their development the support of entities that are, so to speak, 'above' them. Thus, in order to flourish, a person ordinarily needs the help of the family, which in turn needs various kinds of support from the wider community, including the support of its political and social institutions, including the state. Looked at in this way, the principle of subsidiarity draws attention to the responsibilities that a society has to help its members achieve their potential in fullest measure.

However, an equally important aspect of the principle is that a higher body should not take over what can be done by a lower. The *Compendium* quotes *Quadragesimo anno*:

> *Just as it is gravely wrong to take from individuals what they can accomplish by their own initiative and industry and give it to the community, so also it is an injustice and at the same time a grave evil and disturbance of right order to assign to a greater and higher association what lesser and subordinate organisations can do. For every social activity ought of its very nature to furnish help to the members of the body social, and never destroy and absorb them.*[5]

The principle of subsidiarity is generally acknowledged to be one of the most valuable contributions of Roman Catholicism to modern socio-political thought. At first its scope was confined to intra-state political and social activity, but in time, and decisively in the social encyclicals of John XXIII, Paul VI and John Paul II, it was taken to apply also to international relations. Probably the best-known application of the idea in a wider context in modern Europe is its adoption as a principle of the law of the European Union.

OPTIONS

A fifth principle of Catholic social teaching is what it calls a preferential option for the poor. In the *Compendium* this is treated along with the universal destination of goods and is dealt with relatively briefly, but one ought not to conclude from this that it is anything less than central in a Christian vision of the work of justice; and indeed the *Compendium* says that it is to be 'reaffirmed in all its force'. What it means is that, following the example of Jesus, a special attention must be given to the needs of all in our societies who are comprehended by the term 'marginalised'. The *Compendium* elucidates:

> This is an option, or a *special form* of primacy in the exercise of Christian charity, to which the whole tradition of the Church bears witness. It affects the life of each Christian inasmuch as he or she seeks to imitate the life of Christ, but it applies equally to our *social responsibilities* and hence to our manner of living, and to the logical decisions to be made concerning the ownership and use of goods.[6]

As is usual, the *Compendium* makes it clear that the Church's mission is not to establish a particular political or economic order, nor does it envisage only material deprivation. As regards material poverty and deprivation:

> Christian realism, while appreciating on the one hand the praiseworthy efforts being made to defeat poverty, is cautious on the other hand regarding ideological positions and messianistic beliefs that

sustain the illusion that it is possible to eliminate the problem of poverty completely from this world.[7]

Yet the duty to come to the aid of the poor is urgent and grave, and 'Our Lord warns us that we shall be separated from him if we fail to meet the serious needs of the poor and the little ones who are his brethren'. Quoting the Scripture and St Gregory the Great as well as the *Catechism* and the Second Vatican Council, the Compendium insists on the inextricability of the love commandment and the demands of justice:

> When we attend to the needs of those in want, we give them what is theirs, not ours. More than performing works of mercy, we are paying a debt of justice ... [and] ... what is already due in justice is not to be offered as a gift of charity.[8]

Nor is the practice of charity limited to the giving of alms; rather it 'implies addressing the social and political dimensions of the problem of poverty'.

What we have in Catholic social teaching then is both a vision of the human and a corpus of principles whose intent is to promote that vision and translate it into practice. A reader whose first encounter with it is in these pages may already have been struck by the fact that it has been set out here in almost wholly secular terms. Indeed it is a feature of the teaching that it can be so expressed, and a feature of mainline Christian theology, which sees rational reflection on the experience of being human as a valid approach to the discovery of moral truth.

CAN WE TALK?

An obvious advantage is that Catholic social teaching offers the makings of a language with which Christians can dialogue with those who do not share a Christian world-view. Thus it was that Pope John XXIII was confident that the message of *Pacem in terris* could be understood and supported by people of good will outside of the Catholic Church. A disadvantage may be that it could lose touch with theological and especially biblical foundations that give it an enlivening distinctiveness and that can be a powerful source of motivation.

A point sometimes made also is that it is misleading to think of universally held and rationally agreed ideas of what is 'human'. Consider the differences between Western feminist understandings of women's rights and some whose origin is in a Middle Eastern culture. Nor need we suppose that people of good will everywhere agree upon the *content* of individual rights: one has only to reflect on the differences there are about the content of the right to life. In these matters it is well to bear in mind that facile assumptions about commonalities can be as damaging to mutual understanding as can differences.

However, this can be overstated, and is perhaps overstated in some recent writing. It is not a small achievement that so many of the world's peoples can subscribe to the two great Covenants on human rights, as well as numerous conventions and treaties, whose intent is to realise the aspirations of the UN Declaration of 1948. Differences notwithstanding, there is much in common between peoples as regards what is human and what makes for human flourishing. The post-war history of Europe offers hope, as does, for all its imperfections, the story of the European Union.

OPTIONAL?
Meanwhile a commitment to human rights and to all that can help humanise our world is at the heart of the Church's mission to preach and bear witness to the Gospel of Jesus Christ. The social teaching makes it plain that the work of

justice is not an optional but a central Gospel imperative. Some readers of the *Compendium* will be disappointed that it doesn't include the memorable dictum of the 1971 Synod's Work of Justice: that action on behalf of justice is a constitutive dimension of the work of preaching the Gospel. What the *Compendium* does say may be read as a gloss on the Synod's message.

For the *Compendium* affirms that the Church's social doctrine is both *'an integral part of her evangelising ministry'* and *'itself a valid instrument of evangelisation'* (italics original). Speaking of the 'profound links' that exist between 'evangelisation and human promotion', it recalls words of Pope Paul VI:

> These include links of an anthropological order, because the one who is to be evangelised is not an abstract being but is subject to social and economic questions. They also include links in the theological order, since one cannot dissociate the plan of creation from the plan of Redemption. The latter plan touches the very concrete situations of injustice to be combated and of justice to be restored. They include links of the eminently evangelical order, which is that of charity: how in fact can one proclaim the new commandment without promoting in justice and in peace the true, authentic advancement of man?[9]

And so we may return to Pope Benedict's *Deus caritas est*, where in almost identical terms the connection between justice and *agape* is made. It is mistaken to suggest that this Pope's concern for social justice is any the less pressing than that of his predecessors, as may be seen from a reading of the second part of the encyclical. For him as for them it is not the business of the church qua institution to seek to do the work of politics, though he makes it equally clear that this is a vocation of the lay faithful. But even as regards the church as institution, including the church's magisterium,

> ... she cannot and must not remain on the sidelines in the fight for justice. She has to play her part through rational argument and she has to reawaken the spiritual energy without which justice, which always demands sacrifice, cannot prevail and prosper. A just society must be the achievement of politics, not of the Church. Yet the promotion of justice through efforts to bring about openness of mind and will to the demands of the common good is something which concerns the Church deeply.[10]

How deeply has already been hinted. Though, for Benedict, social justice will never be so completely achieved as to make the work of 'social charity' redundant, men and women who follow the Gospel are called to shape a just society. And that – a point of critical importance – is part of what is meant by *ekklesia*, for

> ... the Church's deepest nature is expressed in her three-fold responsibility: of proclaiming the word of God *(kerygma-martyria)*, celebrating the sacraments *(leitourgia)* and exercising the ministry of charity *(diakonia)*. These duties presuppose each other and are inseparable. For the Church, charity is not a kind of welfare activity which could equally well be left to others, but is a part of her nature, an indispensable expression of her very being.[11]

The language of *Deus est caritas* here as elsewhere is evocative of the world of the scholar, and Pope Benedict's horizons and perspectives are different from those of the composers of the Message of the 1971 Synod on Justice in the World. But it would be hard to find a stronger statement of the unbreakable nexus that Christian theology affirms between the work of justice and the mission of Christ's church.

NOTES

1   The phrase is from the Constitution on the Church in the Modern World of Vatican II.
2   English version published by Veritas, 2005. Students of the *Compendium of the Social Doctrine of the Church* will find invaluable help in four works which are readily accessible: P. Corkery, *A Companion to the Compendium*, Veritas, 2007; K. Himes et al. (eds), *Modern Catholic Social Teaching: Commentaries and Interpretations*, Georgetown University Press, 2005; J.A. Dwyer (ed.), *The New Dictionary of Catholic Social Thought*, Liturgical Press, 1994; D. Dorr, *Option for the Poor: A Hundred Years of Catholic Social Teaching*, Orbis Books, 2001 (4th printing).
3   The *Compendium* is a collection of official church documents of various levels of authority, so what it contains is *magisterial teaching*. The term 'Catholic social thought' is, of course, a wider one, and the works cited in the previous footnote both exemplify and provide references to this. The insistence of some writers on a distinction between 'doctrine' and 'teaching' seems fussy, even when what is at stake is the important distinction between unchanging principle and contextual practical application. It is clear from the *Compendium* that Catholic social teaching at every level contains both immutable principle and what the US bishops have termed 'prudential judgment' as to concrete application. The misunderstanding whereby social teaching is thought not to bind conscience may be due in part to the fact that definitive claims are not made for norms of the order of prudential judgements.
4   Patrick Riordan's *A Grammar of the Common Good* (New York and London: Continuum 2008) is a comprehensive, informative, and readable account.
5   *Compendium*, p. 88.
6   Op. cit., p. 86 (emphasis original).
7   Op. cit., p. 87.
8   Ibid.
9   Op. cit., p. 34
10 *Deus caritas est*, par. 28. For an English text see www.vatican.va/holy_father/benedict_xvi/encyclicals/documents/hf_ben-xvi_enc_20051225_deus-caritas-est_en.html
11 Ibid., p. 25.

6.
Human Rights and Christian Faith[1]

The expression 'human rights' is a slogan of our time. With its companion phrase 'civil rights' it has become part of the currency of a certain kind of conversation: the kind of conversation which is concerned with matters of justice. The phrase is used in discourse at every level, from supreme court to public house. Not surprisingly, it has lost some of its sheen and, in informal converse at least, it is often now used unreflectingly, with little sense of its meaning and less of its history.

The title of this chapter invites us to reflect on the notion of human rights with reference to Christian faith: we are asked, that is, to consider the concept in reference to Christian beliefs about humanity and humanity's world. I shall be saying that one of the advantages of the concept is that it is intelligible to people of other religious traditions and of none. I shall be maintaining also that it is particularly congenial to the Christian moral tradition. Indeed I shall be arguing that a commitment to human rights is required of people who profess allegiance to the Christian way.

THE CONCEPT

'People should get their rights', we often say nowadays, meaning that people should get what is their due. The idea is that certain things are due to people, and that they are entitled to them; and that others should respect that entitlement, and should see to it that people should get what is their due. A right always involves a correlative duty: if something is due to me, it is the duty of some other person or institution to ensure that I get it.

A human right is something which is due to us by virtue solely of the fact that we are human beings. It does not, as other rights do, depend on our being citizens, or on having a domicile somewhere, or on being part of any particular community. As members of a polity we have civil rights under the Constitution and the law. In virtue of baptism, members of the Church have certain ecclesial rights. But the rights which we call human rights are our entitlement simply because we are human beings. Put another way, a human right is our entitlement on the basis of our human nature. That is why human rights are sometimes called natural rights – in an older terminology, matters of the natural law.

THE HISTORY
Talking of justice or of morality in terms of rights is a relatively new development among philosophers and theologians. Simplifying somewhat, you could say that it comes from the seventeenth century. In the middle ages it was more usual to speak of ordinances and obligations laid down by law, divine or human, natural or positive. The emphasis was on the enabling power of the law or of the legislator to confer entitlement. Somewhere between Aquinas and Suarez the emphasis began to shift and, in due course, we find assertions of rights as belonging to the subjects of these rights.

The change may be viewed as a matter of emphasis, for one is looking as it were at two sides of a coin. If I say that each person has a right to life and bodily integrity, I am by the same token saying that the moral law requires respect for life and bodily integrity. Yet the difference of emphasis is an important one because, of course, there are other laws besides the moral; and there have been and are regimes in which the demands and prohibitions of the law of the land impinge more upon the public consciousness than do those of the moral law as such. If a right is thought to be something granted by the law, it is easily thought of as something within the gift of the lawmaker – rather than the property of its subject. There may be confusion between civil and human rights. Certain human rights may not be recognised civilly and for that very reason they may not in practice exist at all.

So to say that something is a human right is to say that it is an entitlement that derives from our humanity and that it does not depend for its validity on the will of a ruler. This ethical insight acquired particular importance against the background of the 'divine right' of king or prince or emperor. For centuries it was possible to invoke the authority of the Church as interpreter of God's law so as to restrain tyrants. However, as this gradually became no longer feasible, people had to look for another standard against which to measure the tyrant's laws. The measure came to be expressed in terms of the subject's 'natural rights'. It is not surprising that, as the eighteenth century drew to a close and France was convulsed in revolution against the *ancien regime*, the leaders of the revolution should have published a Declaration of the Rights of Man and of the Citizen; nor that, two years later in 1791, the founding fathers of the US should have added a Bill of Rights to the Constitution.

Of course, in these new regimes and in the emerging nation-states of the next century or so, sovereignty lay with the people, not with the prince. But it continued to be necessary to acknowledge, and from time to time to seek to vindicate, the natural rights of individuals and of groups. For the spread of democracy was only gradual, and it did not preclude the possibility of tyrannical regimes, as much recent history testifies. Nor did theory and practice always match.

In the US, for example, an individual could seek redress under the Constitution. Yet slavery was not abolished until almost a century after the founding fathers had proclaimed that, among the truths which they held self-evident, was that all are born equal. Elsewhere – for example in Ireland – armed insurrection was necessary for the securing of rights which included fundamental rights. In the Germany of the 1930s, national socialism was able to advance bearing a banner on which racism was emblazoned. Nor was the communist socialism of the Union of Soviet Socialist Republics destined to be noted for its devotion to fundamental freedoms. There was – and is – a distance between the rhetoric of human rights and their realisation in practice.

One of the main obstacles to the universal practical realisation of the principles of human rights was the doctrine of national sovereignty. This doctrine, which flourished in the context of the development of the nation-state, meant that governments were immune to effective scrutiny from outside. Paul Sieghart has put the point as follows:

> Had a well-meaning delegation from abroad called on Chancellor Adolf Hitler in 1936 to complain about the notorious Nürnberg laws, and the manner in which they were being applied to persecute German Jews, the Fuhrer would probably have dismissed such an initiative with the classic phrase of an 'illegitimate interference in the internal affairs of the sovereign German State', pointing out that these laws had been enacted in full accordance with the provisions of the German Constitution, by an assembly constitutionally and legally competent to

enact them, and that neither they nor their application were the concern of any meddling foreigners. And, in international law as it then stood, he would have been perfectly right – and so would Party Secretary-General Josef Stalin have been if a similar delegation had called on him at around the same time to complain about the wholesale liquidation of the kulaks in the Soviet Union.[2]

Only after the end of the Second World War did this state of affairs begin to change. On 26 June 1945, the Charter of the United Nations was adopted in San Francisco. Since 1 January 1942, the Allies had been calling themselves 'the United Nations' and, in the Declaration of the United Nations, the signatory governments had committed themselves to the proposition that ' ... complete victory over their enemies is essential to defend life, liberty, independence and religious freedom, and to preserve human rights and justice in their own lands *as well as other lands*'.[3]

In terms of our theme, Articles 55 and 56 of the Charter are crucial: the first declares the intention of the United Nations to promote, *inter alia*, 'universal respect for, and observance of, human rights and fundamental freedoms for all without distinction as to race, sex, language or religion'; and by the second, all member states bind themselves legally to joint and separate action for the achievement of the Charter's purposes.

THE CODE

What are these rights? About three years later, on 10 December 1948, the United Nations' General Assembly met in Paris and formally adopted the Universal Declaration of Human Rights, '... the first complete and detailed catalogue of human rights and fundamental freedoms to be recognised and solemnly declared by the international community of sovereign states'.[4] So began the elaboration of a code of international law, comprising at present two Declarations, two Covenants, three Conventions, including the Convention on the Rights of the Child, and three Charters, together with twenty or so specialised treaties which deal with individual rights or clusters of rights.

It would be pointless here to try to recite the rights thus recognised; what I hope to do, rather, is to offer some general remarks on their character and derivation. But as a matter of interest the most basic and most commonly invoked rights were enumerated on Trócaire's Lenten campaign box some years ago:

> Everyone is born free and equal in dignity and rights. All have the right to: life, freedom and security; food, clothes, shelter and decent living standards; education, work, rest, health services; join a union and enjoy culture; freedom of movement; thought and religion; a fair trial; be considered innocent until proven guilty; join peaceful groups and attend meetings; vote and take part in public life.

Special mention is made of the principle that '... prisoners must be treated humanely and protected from torture, slavery and forced labour ...'.

The ultimate derivation of our human rights is, of course, our common humanity; their ultimate basis the human nature which we all share. One difficulty immediately presents itself: there are differing views upon what constitutes our common humanity; not everyone is agreed upon what is fundamental in human nature.

CRITERIA

This difficulty ought not to be exaggerated for, as the various codes testify, there is quite a consensus upon the enumeration of individual rights. There is a notable measure of agreement also upon the criteria by which rights may be identified, and the following account is fairly representative:

> As the notion 'human rights' has come to be understood in contemporary international usage, it means a set of justifiable or legitimate claims with at least six features: (1) they impose duties of performance or forbearance upon all appropriately situated human beings, including governments; (2) they are possessed equally by all human beings regardless of laws, customs or agreements; (3) they are of basic importance to human life; (4) they are properly sanctionable and enforceable upon default by legal means; (5) they have special presumptive weight in constraining human action; and (6) they include a certain number that are considered inalienable, indefensible and unforfeitable.[5]

Plainly, the second and third of these characteristics of a human right are the most fundamental: that human rights are concerned with goods which are of basic importance in human life, and that they are possessed equally by all human beings. Close to these in significance is the sixth: that the rights which we call human rights include some that are inalienable, indefeasible and unforfeitable. Indeed it is sometimes said that the special properties of truly human rights are that they are 'inherent', 'inalienable' and 'equal'. We have already seen something of what it means to say that a right is inherent: we are born with it, we do not need to acquire it, it is not anyone's gift to us, it is ours simply because we are. A human right is inalienable: it cannot be taken from us, nor can we give it away or otherwise dispose of it.

The first, fourth and fifth characteristics can be grouped together too, beginning with the proposition that human rights '... impose duties of performance or forbearance on all appropriately situated human beings ...'. This is simply saying that every right imposes a corresponding duty on someone; and this is a point to which we must return. Of course, as we have seen, a human right is in the first place a moral reality. It might not, in point of fact, be accorded someone in a given situation, and so, as the fourth criterion states, rights must be '... sanctionable and enforceable upon default by legal means ...'

One of the major achievements of our time is the extent to which this requirement has become realisable, at least in principle, as more and more states have bound themselves by the code of which I spoke earlier.

The fifth characteristic, that human rights have '... special presumptive weight in constraining human action ...' means, broadly speaking, that the onus of justification is on anyone who seeks to curtail or frustrate such a right. Of course, we have already seen above that there are some rights that are inalienable and indefeasible, and so may never be fustrated or curtailed. These include the prohibition against slavery and against 'cruel, inhuman or degrading treatment or punishment', and the requirements for a fair trial.

It can be seen at once that while the second and third characteristics are the most fundamental, they are also the characteristics that may give rise to differences of viewpoint, for not everyone is agreed upon what is of basic importance in human life; nor is it clear that what is thought basic belongs equally to everyone. I said earlier that this point should not be exaggerated, and that there is a very great consensus in regard to the listing of basic rights. In this context, it is useful to employ the distinction suggested by some commentators between 'generations' of rights.

The first generation of human rights, those which historically were the first to be classified as human rights, are, in general, certain basic freedoms of civil or political import: freedom from torture – to choose first a negative example; or freedom of association or of speech – to mention positive rights. The second generation was associated with the thought of Marx and the rise of socialism, and they refer to certain prerequisites of the exercise of any freedoms. So, for example, rights began to be recognised in respect of health care, work, housing and education, these being seen as prerequisites of human flourishing and conditions for the exercise of first-generation rights. The third generation has been emerging since the 1960s, associated especially with the 'developing nations'. These amount to claims to certain basic needs of living, such as water, food, shelter.

PRACTICE

As mentioned earlier, among the characteristics of a human right according to the description offered by Childress and Macquarrie is that it is sanctionable and enforceable by legal means. Another word for this characteristic is 'justiciable'. And it is interesting that in standard treatment of human rights, whereas those of the first generation are held to be on the whole justiciable, those of the second and third are less obviously so. What is to be regarded as 'due' living accommodation, for example, and whose duty is it to ensure that everyone is so accommodated? Against whom would an action lie were one to seek to vindicate a right to shelter or housing? And what of a right to food or drink? The fact that the answers to such questions are less than self-evident has made the justiciability of these rights problematic. It has also afforded a cover for regimes which, while nominally subscribing to the code, are negligent in respect of the goods to which these rights refer.

We can only be glad that most modern states are party to one or another of the instruments that make up our contemporary code of human rights. Of course, one might formally subscribe to a code and nevertheless violate it, and we have just seen that it is quite possible to do this with impunity in regard to rights which are not justiciable, or not obviously so. It is possible also to do so in the case of some justiciable rights for, apart from the case of those which are inalienable and indefeasible, it is usual to write into constitutions, and other laws, clauses allowing for the limitation of rights, and even for their suspension in situations of emergency.

This is standard practice and is indeed a necessary feature of the business of lawmaking, for the law has to regulate the exercise of rights and freedoms in such a way as to facilitate the maximum common good. However, the limitations that the law imposes, and especially those that involve the suspension or curtailment of rights in emergency situations, must be scrutinised carefully lest they be used in an unjust way. Again, a concern for human rights must make us look to our own community as well as to those communities which are the objects of contemporary fashionable benevolence.

THE CHURCH AND HUMAN RIGHTS

So far we have been talking about human rights in wholly secular terms. This has not been because of a literal-minded adherence to the order of words in our chapter title, 'Human Rights and Christian Faith', but rather in order to bring out an important point. That is, that it is in fact possible to speak of human rights in wholly secular terms; and this can only be advantageous in a world where we must make common cause with people whose ethical idiom is not that of the Christian religion, indeed not religious at all.

As a matter of interest, the Church – conceived as a community of believers – has at no time been the sole instrument in the development of either the theory or the practice of human rights: indeed it has often apparently been an opponent of this manner of thinking and talking. There have been two main reasons for this. The first is that many of the movements that advocated the rights of man, going back to the French Revolution, were anti-religious and Church leadership feared that the apparently individualistic emphases of the new social doctrine would lead people away from true Christianity. The second reason is that 'the Church' was itself in many ways a part of the prevailing social systems. Its leadership was quite often privileged, as were its most influential lay members. It is naturally difficult to espouse a cause whose *raison d'être* appears to be the subversion of one's own traditional status.[6]

Yet in another sense the Church was an instrument of the changes, for it had been the custodian of the natural law tradition, out of which rights doctrine came. More basically still, the Judaeo-Christian religious tradition was itself the repository of certain ideas about what it means to be a human being which, over a long period and often in face of great difficulty, worked themselves into the European mind. In the very birth of the movement for human rights, the framers of the American Declaration of Independence felt bound to ascribe these rights to the endowment of the Creator; and even the French Revolution, ostensibly rejecting God in the name of reason, nevertheless when it wished to point to the superior and ultimate character of the rights which it proclaimed, could not avoid the religious word 'sacred'.

In any case, resistance in the Church to ideas associated with rights theory turned in time to wholehearted endorsement. From Leo XIII, in his encyclical *Rerum novarum* a hundred years ago, the Popes have repeatedly called attention to human rights generally and individually. And in many parts of the world Church leaders have been to the fore – sometimes at great cost – in the work of promoting rights, and of defending them, particularly in the case of those who are especially vulnerable.

HUMAN RIGHTS AND CHRISTIAN FAITH

Such development in the Church's stance on human rights was inevitable, given the nature of the Christian faith. For human rights are founded in the dignity of each human being, a dignity which is acknowledged even in a non-religious view of life, but whose recognition is *demanded* by the Christian view. Christians believe that God has created us in His own image. This gives humans a dignity more enhanced than reason can tell. Sin dims God's image in us, but we do not forfeit our dignity; for grace is restored to us through what was done in Jesus Christ.

In the Christian view, too, each of us is brother or sister. Acknowledging a common Father we may see rights as the attributes of the humanity of the sister or the brother. And so we may experience our obligations not in cold justice but in love. Another way of looking at this is as follows. Love is the core commandment of the Christian way, but love requires expression in concrete terms. It is expressed in a respect for life which seeks to promote a quality of life and not merely the conditions of minimal survival. It is expressed in a regard for truthfulness and its associated virtues, such as honour and integrity and fidelity. It is expressed in the pursuit of justice, in the securing and guaranteeing of the range of specific rights that international opinion is gradually recognising and endorsing. So the Christian commandment to love requires commitment to the promotion of human rights. One cannot be a Christian without a wholehearted commitment to the securing and defence of human rights for all.

The Christian faith is based on a gospel that speaks of the inbreak of the reign of God in the world. That reign was anticipated in the Old Testament expectation of an era in which swords would be beaten into ploughshares, the lion would lie down with the lamb, and justice and peace would rule upon the earth. The Christian gospel is that that era was inaugurated in the life and work of Jesus Christ and that it will be completed when He comes again. Meanwhile those who follow the way of Jesus are called to share in the work of building up the rule of God. Faith and hope in the gospel call us forward to cooperate in the work of freeing humankind to be fully human. Which is another way to say that Christain faith calls us to defend and promote human rights.

NOTES

1   Pauline Berwick and Margaret Burns (eds), *The Rights of The Child: Irish Perspectives on the UN Convention*, Council for Social Welfare, 1991.
1   Paul Sieghart, *The Lawful Rights of Mankind: An Introduction to the International Legal Code of Human Rights*, Oxford: 1985, p. vii.
2   *Everyman's United Nations: A Complete Handbook of the Activities and Evolution of the United Nations During the First Twenty Years* (1945–1965), New York, 1968, p. 6 (emphasis added).
3   Sieghart, op. cit., p. 63.
4   J. Childress and J. Macquarrie (eds), *A New Dictionary of Christian Ethics*, London, 1985, p. 279.
5   It is probably unnecessary to observe that this obstacle has not disappeared.

7.
Christian Values in a Pluralist Society

A few years ago the title of this paper would probably have suggested a reflection on morality and law in the context of Church–State relations in Ireland, and the Church most prominently in question was the Roman Catholic. For we had grown accustomed to recurrent public debate about the embodiment of certain moral beliefs in the law of the land, and the focal question usually was whether it was appropriate that, in an increasingly pluralist society, moral beliefs associated especially (and sometimes exclusively) with the Catholic Church should in effect be imposed on people not of that faith.

Most of the controversies of the past few decades have been settled: the 'special position' of the Catholic Church accorded by the Constitution – for what in any case it meant – is a dim memory, the laws that reflected Catholic teaching on contraception have gone and there is no longer a constitutional prohibition on divorce legislation.[1] Further, the potential for influence of the leadership of the Church has apparently been diminished, partly because of the scandals that have beset the Church over the past decade; partly also because of the decline in church membership which appears to have taken hold during the same period; partly, finally, owing to an increasingly evident pluralism of religious belief and practice.

So the title of this chapter now bespeaks a different kind of reflection, or rather a reflection in different terms.

For the question is no longer primarily that of the influence of the institutional Church or Churches upon the institutions of the State, but the influence of Christianity in the shaping of Irish society. I do not mean to say that the Church as an institution can have no influence in that process; indeed I shall maintain later that it can and should. However, the Church is in the first place the community of believers in the way of the Lord Jesus. It is through the life and activity of the members of that community that Christian values and the Christian vision for human living will be mediated to future generations.

It was inevitable, though also misleading, that the question should in the past have been framed in terms of Church–State relations. It was inevitable because there were in fact discernible traces of Catholic influence in the Constitution of 1937 and in various legislation since the foundation of the State in 1922. On the whole, people were content to leave direction on moral questions to the leaders of the Church, as they were law to the leaders of the State. It was, however, also misleading, for it masked the fact that at the core of each debate was an issue with which every society has to contend: how to reconcile individual freedoms with the claims of a common welfare. It tended to mask, too, the truth that responsibility for the moral future of Ireland lies in the conscience of every citizen of whatever religious persuasion.

There are advantages and opportunities in the changed situation. There is the challenge now of recognising that responsibility for the preservation of moral values lies not just with the leaders of the Churches or of the State but with each citizen. There is an opportunity to take seriously the point that morality is concerned not just with a handful of issues of sexual ethics, but with the whole spectrum of our relationships with each other and with the world which we inhabit. At another level we are coming to see that we are now part of the larger community of Europe, indeed of the world, and that our moral agenda is no longer merely domestic.

THE CHALLENGES

More than forty years ago the Second Vatican Council described the modern situation in terms whose truth has been endorsed by all that has happened since, and which remain an apt account of today's world:

> Ours is a new age of history with profound and rapid changes spreading gradually to all corners of the earth. They are the products of people's intelligence and creative activity, but they recoil upon them, upon their judgements and desires, both individual and collective, upon their ways of thinking and acting in regard to people and things. We are entitled then to speak of a real social and cultural transformation whose repercussions are felt at the religious level also.[2]

Advances in science and technology, all that is involved – economically, politically, socially, culturally – in 'globalisation', the persistence of warfare and the continuing threat of nuclear disaster, various threats to the environment: contexts and background to choices and decisions which will determine the future of humanity and our world.

Ireland, for better and for worse, is in the mainstream of change now, and there is no issue of a global order that will not have an impact, direct or indirect, on us. The problems of 'Europe' are our problems in an unprecedented way, as indeed are the problems of a wider world: think only of the global economic crisis. And we have some characteristic problems of our own. Still with us, for all the astonishing progress that has been made, is the task of building a lasting peace on our island, the achievement of real reconciliation, and the creation of the social conditions in which each man and woman may be assured of respect for their dignity as human beings. This is a task of politics and of politicians, but at its core it's a moral challenge, and responsibility for it lies in the consciences of us all.

There are other problems and challenges. The poor are still with us, their plight the more striking now in the light of the prosperity of the many and the great wealth of a few. In 2006, a Joint Oireachtas Committee reported improvement in the resources available for combating adult illiteracy, which according to a 1997 OECD survey affected about one-quarter of the population. It is plain from the Committee's report that functional illiteracy among adults remains a significant problem. In the Committee's words: 'In a "learning" or "knowledge" society people who lack basic skills are seriously marginalised and disadvantaged, not only in their employment prospects but also in daily, civic and personal life.'[3]

Not that Irish society has been oblivious of these defects, and during the past few decades there have been renewed efforts on the part of the State to alleviate poverty and to help cope with the problems to which poverty gives rise. We have witnessed also an improvement as regards access to education at all levels; and there have been some advances in health care, even if they are scarcely noticeable by the side of scandalous deficiencies; and in the sphere of 'welfare', for all that there remains much to criticise. We have had an impressive contribution from voluntary organisations, whether religious in their inspiration or secular, even when their best efforts are regularly frustrated through lack of funding and other resources.

However, improvement is slow, change often not radical enough and there is evidence of a lack of political will when it comes to any measure that might trouble the more powerful sectors of society.[4] There is evidence also of a detachment – a growing detachment? – on the part of people generally from the problems of those who are on the margins and who remain deprived. It is disquieting to learn that organisations such as the St Vincent de Paul Society and the Simon Community have been encountering difficulty in recruiting volunteers.

The Irish tradition has accorded a special place to hospitality and the kindly treatment of the stranger. It is again disconcerting to witness the ambivalence at an official level, and the hostility and resentment in some localities, in dealing with refugees and asylum-seekers, and indeed migrants generally, during the past few years. Even more ominous are the reports of racist attitudes and reactions in the streets and in particular neighbourhoods. Tourists, expecting to be met with friendliness and courtesy – not to mention fair dealing and value for money – are latterly encountering obnoxious behaviour at the hands of their hosts. Some immigrants have a tale to tell that puts stark questions about our real attitudes to the stranger.[5]

There are issues that arise directly out of our participation in the forging of a European Community. We have been happy to accept the economic benefits that membership of the Community has brought and, on the whole, our participation in the political and administrative structures of the union has been creditable. However, public consciousness of our membership is dominated by the motif of economic benefit, and it will be interesting to see how we react henceforward, now that economic benefit is not so immediate or obvious. During the past few years, voices have been heard among the Union's leaders recalling the vision of the founders, for whom economic cooperation, albeit crucial, was only the basis and starting-point for a social and political cooperation that betokened a real solidarity and a truly human community. It would be strange indeed if we were unable and unwilling to contribute to that task out of the resources bequeathed us by our history and our cultural and spiritual inheritance.

THE LEGACY

Moral values are not abstract; they are embodied in the choices people make. These choices tell more about the actual value system of an individual or a people than do the formal or official accounts to which people profess to subscribe. The vision of life we have inherited is predominantly the Christian, but, of course, it does not follow that the values that have shaped and shape our choices are always the values of Christianity.

There is nothing surprising about this: 'For I do not do the good that I want, but the evil that I do not want is what I do'.[6] Our perceptions, as individuals or as a society, of 'the good that I want' are conditioned by time and place. It is easier in hindsight to see fault and wrong than it is to know what to do in the present and for the future. The shortcomings of Irish Christianity have been all too well documented in the media and in the novels and drama of our time, and it is salutary for Christians to reflect upon, repent and, where possible, atone for the sins of the past. However, it is folly to suppose that the human propensity to do what is good, or our ability to discern what is truly good, is purer, less prone to error and to wilful failure than was the case in past generations. Self-righteousness is never a good starting-point for an attempt to discover and live better ways, and the demonising and scapegoating of individuals or of groups is infantile and unproductive.

I have already made the point that responsibility for the future of moral values rests with each citizen of whatever religious persuasion. Christians who wish to work for the moral betterment of society take their place alongside people of good will who do not share their faith. But Christians are entitled, and by their own faith obliged, to reflect upon the problems of today and tomorrow, in the light of the Christian moral inheritance. What values do Christians profess to cherish and must wish to pass on to the next generation? The Christian gospel is first a religious message: the kingdom of God – the reign of love and justice, grace and peace – has been inaugurated and, in the fullness of time, God will be all in all. This has direct implications for the moral life, the chief of which is that we are to love our neighbour as ourselves. The neighbour is everyone, for we are each made in the image of God and each is brother or sister in the Lord.

The simplicity of the love commandment is, of course, deceptive, for though some of its requirements are almost self-evident, and Christians see them as endorsed by Revelation – respect for life, truthfulness, giving people their rights, looking out for the neighbour in need – it is not always easy in practice to discern the concrete forms of behaviour to which these requirements give rise. The essentials do not change, but the world that the followers of Jesus inhabit is diverse and changing. The Christian tradition has grappled with these questions through the centuries, evolving principles and norms of behaviour that aim to embody the moral vision Jesus taught and lived. The community of Christian believers has also tried to live up to that vision, or live it, sometimes successfully, sometimes not. So it is with the community of Christians today.

Our time professes to place a special value on the dignity of the human being; and we speak also of equality, and of the value of freedom as a constitutive element of human dignity. And we have come to speak of 'human rights' – entitlements which belong to everyone by virtue simply of being human and which must be respected, and guaranteed and vindicated by the law. The Christian moral tradition is on the whole content to adopt the concept and the language of human rights in order to express the concrete demands of right moral living. It is aware of the danger of a certain individualist bias in rights discourse and in their pursuit, and seeks to counter it by an insistence on correlative responsibilities, and by emphasising the need to recognise that we are persons-in-community, and the virtue of neighbourly solidarity.

In their commitment to notions such as human dignity and equality and in their recognition of the claims expressed as human rights, conscientious Christians can feel at one with conscientious people of other religions and of none. They can make common cause with people not of their faith in the struggle to secure the human rights of those who are deprived of them. The Church in the modern world can, as the Second Vatican Council put it, share the joy and hope as well as the grief and anguish of every man and woman of our time.[7] There are commonalities as well as pluralism of moral value, in Ireland as elsewhere, and the differences between (and among) Christians and others ought not to be exaggerated.

A SPECIFICALLY CHRISTIAN CONTRIBUTION?

Can Christians bring anything in particular to the task of creating Ireland's future? During the past few decades there has been a debate among theologians as to what, if anything, differentiates the morality of Christian faith from that of other people. The debate has hinged upon the question whether there is anything in the *content* of Christian morality that cannot be discerned from a reasoned reflection on what it is to be a human being in the world. Contributors to the discussion are agreed that

Christian faith furnishes a vision of life, within which we make our moral choices and which influences the choices we make. It is also agreed that the Christian faith-vision offers a distinctive and enhanced motivation for moral living: a Christian professes to behave rightly towards the fellow human being not only because the other is equal in dignity but because he or she is brother or sister in the Lord. All recognise the powerful exemplary significance of the way in which Jesus lived and died. The difference between them is on the question whether there are concrete norms of behaviour which can be known only from Revelation and in faith.

The detail of the debate and its present status need not concern us here.[8] For our purposes it is perhaps enough to say this: whatever the differences or commonalities between the morality of the Christian and that of others, the profession of Christianity in any case commits one to certain perspectives on human living, and it commits one to certain kinds of choices. The Christian believes in a creator-God, whose creation reflects the goodness and beauty of the divine, and of whom the human person is an image. This God is trinitarian and the image of God in us is relational, so that in our deepest nature we are persons-in-community.

The Christian's picture of life includes an acknowledgement of sin and sinfulness, personal, social and structural. It does not minimise what is nowadays called the dark side of human nature and human existence. It acknowledges that at best our motivations are mixed, our achievements imperfect, our best constructs flawed. However, it trusts also in the hope of salvation, for the individual and for the world, which is disclosed in the death and resurrection of Jesus the Christ. And its focus upon Jesus as the Way, the Truth and the Life entails commitment to the love-commandment as it was taught and lived by him.

In the disclosure of the dimensions of the love-commandment in the preaching and life of Jesus there is an unmistakable bias towards the neighbour who is in need – towards the people on the margins, as they are often called today. The tone is set in Luke's account of the beginning of Jesus' ministry in Galilee, as Jesus visits the synagogue of his youth and unrolls the scroll and finds where it is written: 'the Spirit of the Lord is upon me, because he has anointed me to bring the good news to the poor. He has sent me to proclaim release to the captives and recovery of sight to the blind, to let the oppressed go free, to proclaim the year of the Lord's favour'.[9] 'Today this scripture has been fulfilled in your hearing.'[10]

The impact and significance of Jesus' meeting with the woman at the well is underestimated if we are not aware of certain prejudices of his time and place.[11] The choice of a Samaritan as a model of neighbourly behaviour towards the man who fell among robbers had to be startling to an audience for whom the Samaritans were enemy.[12] The renunciation of any kind of temporal power and of coercion in the fulfilment of his destiny as Messiah was shocking to people who looked for political deliverance and an earthly kingdom. Jesus' acceptance of death on a cross was a scandal and a folly.[13]

It is not, therefore, a merely transient incident of contemporary Christianity that the faith of the Christian should impel to active concern for the poor and to transformative action in aid of the dignity, equality and entitlement to the human rights of everyone, especially of the people of the margins. In words of the Synod on Justice in the World in 1971: 'Action on behalf of justice and participation in the transformation of the world fully appear to us [the Pope and the bishops of the world gathered in synod] as a constitutive dimension of the preaching of the Gospel, or, in other words, of the Church's mission for the redemption of the human race and its liberation from every oppressive situation.'[14] This is the consistent message also of the social teaching of Pope John Paul II.[15]

There is, of course, more to be said about the Christian understanding of the moral life than that it involves what is nowadays called a preferential option for the poor. One might, for example, speak of the radicality and generosity of moral response that is called for in the Sermon on the Mount.[16] One might reflect on the implications of the biblical concepts of morality as discipleship or as imitation of Christ. One might refer to the fact that in Christian theology 'to imitate and live out the love of Christ is not possible for man by his own strength alone. He becomes *capable of this love only by virtue of a gift received*'.[17] And one might raise the question of the relationship between Christian spirituality, including prayer and sacramental worship, and a conscious living out of the Christian moral vision.

These themes are beyond the scope of this piece, the main concern of which is to suggest what, at least in general terms, adherents of the Christian tradition might contribute to promoting and sustaining moral value in Ireland in the new millennium. It is an important part of my case that responsibility rests with each Christian and that the values of the Gospel will be realised only insofar as they inform and inspire the decisions and choices that Christians make. Of course, it may also be expected that the Churches as institutions will continue to play a part. I am thinking mainly of my own Church, so it is perhaps all the more necessary to make the point that common sense, not to mention their common commitment to the core values of the Christian message, suggests that the time is ripe for exploring ways in which the Christian Churches might cooperate among themselves, as well as with people of other faiths, in the task of shaping the Ireland of the future.

CHURCH AND SOCIETY IN THE FUTURE

The dimensions of the changes that have been taking place in the Catholic Church in Ireland during the past decade and a half are not yet fully clear, nor is their full significance for the task of leadership in the Church and in society. The anger and disillusionment that have followed disclosure of the various scandals have taken their toll on Church attendance and on people's readiness to listen to the Church's leaders when moral issues are addressed. No doubt also we have been influenced by the secularising impetus that seems endemic in postmodern western European culture. The internal tensions and polarisations that have latterly marked the Catholic Church generally can be found in Ireland too. The challenge to the Church and its leadership, in terms of effective witness to and proclamation of the Gospel, is complex and daunting.

Liam Ryan has proposed that as regards the relationship between the Church and society in the future, the role of the Church might be that of conscience of society.[18] This idea was taken up by Enda McDonagh who, whilst granting its merit, raised some questions:

> Is the Church the only conscience of society? Who as Church shall speak for the conscience of society? Is this a task for the bishops only, or bishops and priests, or the laity? Is it an ecumenical task for the Churches working together, or one for the Catholic Church only? On what issues shall this conscience be voiced, on the traditional issues of sexual morality, respect for life in terms of abortion or political violence, on education, or is there a whole wider range of issues? How are these issues discerned? How are conscience judgements formed about them? Who shall listen to this conscience? How shall its judgement be offered or imposed?[19]

Ryan's suggestion and McDonagh's questions are perhaps even more apt now than when first made, and they intimate the complexity of the Church's task. The questions are a good description of the agenda that must be tackled by Church leaderships that wish to influence Irish society as it seeks to articulate a value system for the times ahead. Some, of course, will want to say that these questions belong to the past, that the Churches as institutions have lost their footing irretrievably. How can someone be a 'conscience' until his own house is put in order? Trust lost is painfully difficult to regain, when it can be regained at all.

Yet there are, as I said earlier, advantages and opportunities in the situation that has emerged in Ireland and, in terms of the Catholic Church's self-understanding and its own spiritual and moral vision, there are some specific advantages and opportunities. We are in a time of fresh insight into the Gospel truth that the Son of Man came not to be served but to serve.[20] It is a time of insight, too, into the truth that 'My kingdom is not from this world'.[21] There is a challenge to a deeper understanding of the injunction of Jesus: 'Do this in remembrance of me.'[22] It is possible to hope for a renewal of the Church as institution, not only in aid of the faith and hope of its own membership, but also the better to fit it for its Gospel call to be a leaven in society and a light in the world.

NOTES

1　Abortion is, of course, a critically important exception and there has also been some public discussion of the law on euthanasia. The response of the Bishops' Conference to any proposals concerning the law in these areas will doubtless be informed by the teaching of Pope John Paul's encyclical *Evangelium vitae*. See especially paragraphs 68–74. Tr. Veritas, 1995, pp. 124–37.

2　*Gaudium et spes*, par. 4. Tr. A. Flannery (ed.), *Vatican Council II. Constitutions, Decrees, Declarations*, Dublin and New York, 1996.

3　Houses of the Oireachtas, Joint Committee on Education and Science, Fourth Report: Adult Literacy in Ireland, May 2006, 2.1.4.

4　A majority of the Constitutional Review Group rejected the suggestion that economic and social rights might be included in a revised Constitution: see *Report of the Constitution Review Group*, May 1996, Government Publications, pp. 234–6. There are obvious difficulties but none that is obviously insuperable. The case for inclusion of rights to health, adequate housing, adequate nutrition and an adequate standard of living is argued in *Re-righting the Constitution*, published in 1998 by the Irish Commission for Justice and Peace. This is the product of a process that involved written and oral submissions to the All Party Committee for the Review of the Constitution, and it includes a response to the main objections and difficulties raised in the Review Group's *Report*.

5　See, for example, Chichi Aniagolu, 'Being Black in Ireland', in Ethel Crowley and Jim MacLaughlin (eds), *Under the Belly of the Tiger: Class, Race, Identity and Culture in the Global Ireland*, Dublin, 1997. Also Fintan Farrell and Philip Watt (eds), *Responding to Racism in Ireland*, Dublin, 2001.

6　Romans 7:19. The translation used throughout is the *New Revised Standard Version* (Catholic Edition), London, 1993.

7　*Gaudium et spes*, Preface.

8　See Vincent Macnamara, 'The Distinctiveness of Christian Morality' in Bernard Hoose (ed.), *Christian Ethics*, London, 1998, p. 149ff.

9　Lk 4:18,19.

10　Ibid.

11　Jn 4:1-30.

12　Lk 10:25-37.

13　I Cor 1:23.

14　*Justice in the World*, Synod of Bishops 1971, tr. A. Flannery (ed.), *Vatican Council II: More Post-Conciliar Documents*, Dublin, 1982, p. 696.

15　See especially *Centesimus Annus*, tr. Veritas, Dublin, 1991; also *Tertio Millenio Adveniente*, especially pars 11–13, London, 1994.

16   Mt 5-7. Cf. Lk 6, 11, 12. Commenting on the moral teaching of the
     Sermon, 'the magna charta of Gospel morality', Pope John Paul II
     wrote: *Jesus brings God's commandments to fulfilment*,
     particularly the commandment of love of neighbour, *by
     interiorising their demands and by bringing out their fullest
     meaning*. Love of neighbour springs from *a loving heart* which,
     precisely because it loves, is ready to live out *the loftiest
     challenges*. Jesus shows that the commandments must not be
     understood as a minimum limit not to be gone beyond, but rather
     as a path involving a moral and spiritual journey towards
     perfection, at the heart of which is love (cf. Col 3:14)'. *Veritatis
     splendor*, par. 15. Tr. as in John Wilkins (ed.), *Understanding
     Veritatis splendor*, London, 1994, pp. 94, 95. Original emphasis.
17   Op. cit., p. 101.
18   'The Church in Politics', *The Furrow* 30 (1979), No. 1, p. 17.
19   Enda McDonagh, *The Making of Disciples*, Dublin, 1982, p. 177.
20   Mk 10:45.
21   Jn 18:36.
22   Lk 22:19.

8.
Sharia?

A decade ago the term *Sharia* would probably have meant nothing to a majority of the population of this island and much the same could be said of Britain. If this is still true it is not the fault of the media on either island, for the term figures regularly in coverage of matters Islamic, and Islam is nowadays rarely out of the news. It doesn't follow that the concept of Sharia is any the better understood, of course, as the public controversy that followed a recent lecture by the Archbishop of Canterbury has shown.[1]

The Archbishop's focal topic was Islam in English Law and he gave the lecture in the Royal Courts of Justice in London to an audience made up mainly of lawyers. The concerns he addressed, explicit and underlying, go far beyond the realm of law and the interest of English lawyers. For the lecture touched on questions that are central in the practice and theory of politics on all of the continents, not least in those which at present most impinge on these islands, namely Europe and the United States. If warrant is needed for introducing such concerns in these pages, one need go no further than to quote Dr Williams' closing thought: 'Theology still waits for us around the corner of these debates.'

The cause of the controversy is itself a question of theology, for it concerns the meaning for Muslims of Sharia law. That question is current in Britain and elsewhere for a few reasons. First, there is at least a perception that Muslim communities are answerable to Sharia before they are answerable to the law of the land. Related to this is an impression that the Muslim faith insists on the replacement everywhere of secular laws by a Sharia system. A third reason is that what the term evokes for many unschooled in Islam is the spectre of harsh punishment for violation of Sharia provisions, most notably in the area of sexual ethics. A fourth reason is a fear that any gains in the direction of equality that women in western societies have latterly made must surely be jeopardised should Sharia be given a footing.

Against this background it is not surprising that when Archbishop Williams, referring especially to Sharia and the law of the United Kingdom, posed the question whether secular law needs to accommodate some of the religious ordinances of faith communities, there ensued, as they say, a storm of protest. Some of the protest can be disposed of by invoking, as Dr Williams later did, a description by Ronald Knox of a student debate in Oxford: 'The prevailing attitude … was one of heavy disagreement with a number of things which [the speaker] had not said.' There was disagreement also, however, about things that the Archbishop *had* said and the critics were by no means all of the stamp of Alf Garnett. Nevertheless he reiterated and defended his position, clarifying points he thought had been distorted in public discussion.

It would be folly to attempt a summary of a dense and nuanced presentation and one is mindful that it was a failure to appreciate nuance that led some of the Archbishop's critics into ill-judged rejoinders. Yet it is fair to say that a core issue was the question whether it is possible or desirable for UK law to accommodate some Sharia provisions. After all, the law in England already incorporates the canon law of the Church of England as regards church property and appointments (and this is to say nothing of what is involved in Establishment). Moreover, there is an accommodation of Jewish law in the civil recognition of the findings of a Beth Din, a court to which Jewish men and women may have recourse on certain matters of marriage and family law. Indeed there is already some accommodation to Sharia law itself, in the availability now of mortgage and investment systems designed in view of Sharia's prohibition of the taking of interest on a loan.

The plausibility of the Archbishop's question – and in the brouhaha it was forgotten that he was putting a question rather than contending for a particular conclusion – must depend in great part, obviously, on the validity of the perceptions and fears already mentioned. Is it true that for a Muslim *Sharia* furnishes the ultimate and decisive ordinance? Is it true that Islam enjoins the universal dominion of *Sharia* law? What about the punishments – mutilation and even death – whose incidence in some of the countries in which *Sharia* prevails cannot be gainsaid? What *is* the *Sharia*'s view of women and women's role?

Archbishop Williams did not purport to offer a detailed account of the nature of Sharia, wisely of course, for a detailed treatment, even if within a commentator's competence, would require more than a lecture or an article. *Sharia* for a Muslim is indeed God's will and it encompasses all of the believer's duties to God and humanity and humanity's abode, and it is the standard by which everything human is judged. Its sources are acknowledged by all Muslims to be the Koran and the *Sunna*, which is the name for the pattern of life as well as the teaching of the Prophet, access to which is by way of authentic and authoritative 'report' (*Hadith*).

However, the question of what to make of those sources, how they are to be understood and appropriated from age to age and from place to place, is the subject of a complex jurisprudence (*Fiqh*) and has given rise to schools of interpretation whose approaches and methodologies differ. Even within the schools there is a spectrum of theological standpoint and viewpoint that ranges from 'traditionalist' to 'reformist', from 'liberal' to 'fundamentalist', from 'fideist' to 'rationalist' – to make use of terms that are as unsatisfactory as they are, it seems, unavoidable.

The response that a Muslim may give to the questions and fears listed earlier will be shaped by his or her tradition and by the experience of the faith-community into which the believer was born. Like the faith of the other two Abrahamic religions, the faith of Islam is an embodied faith, open, therefore, to the influences of history, geography, economics and politics, and the exigencies of life in a swiftly changing world. The texts of Islam can be used to dominate and destroy, but so can the Books and traditions of its Jewish and Christian antecedents: 'The devil can cite scripture for his purpose.' All the more reason for continuous respectful conversation now among people of good will who belong to those faiths and with people who hold what is usually (if perhaps misleadingly) called a secularist vision of the good life.

So it is that inter-church dialogue, interfaith dialogue and a dialogue with secular humanism are no mere fads of a 'postmodern' time and frame of mind. So it is that Archbishop Williams' reflections and the reception they received have a significance that goes far beyond their immediate context and purview. So it is that on this island we have our own reflection to do and our own conversations to hold, even if in a context very different from that to which Dr Williams spoke, and from a very different religious history.

Our reflection has already begun, of course, and there are also conversations, including conversations with Islam. A cynic might say that it is obviously time for reflection and conversation when we have 35,000 Muslims in our midst; when their contribution to business and the professions and the work-force generally is unmissable now; when their children need to be educated in a system that in so many ways has been unprepared; when their sick and elderly and disadvantaged have as good a call on our society's strained resources as does any citizen. A cynic might also observe that it is no wonder that religious leaders should – at last – make common cause, when the practice of religion and its prospects have undergone such swift and drastic change.

Yet, though it would be foolish to deny anomalies, it is no small matter that the Irish Constitution affords a guarantee of our law's respect for all religions; that no religion is to be privileged; that the State may not coerce religious practice or impose a religious belief. It is no small matter that we have placed ourselves within the reach of the law of the European Union and of international human rights law, again granted anomalies and shortcomings about which no one need be complacent. Nor should we make little of the fact that there is now the possibility of 'structured dialogue' between the civil authorities and the leaders of churches, faith communities and non-confessional bodies.

Where this will lead, in terms of the values and expectations of Irish Muslims, remains, of course, to be seen. Much will depend on leadership. Participation in the dialogues must present a special challenge to the leaders of what is still the majority church.

A clue to what will count with the Muslim community may be found in words of Ali Selim, General Secretary to the Irish Council of Imams, calling for commitment of church leaders to the creation, as a matter of urgency, of 'sound inter-faith relations'. The appointment of Archbishop Brady to the College of Cardinals, he wrote, 'renowned for his personal integrity, kindness, goodness and his hand of friendship across communities, could provide a new avenue in this context'. And Archbishop Diarmuid Martin, by visiting the Islamic Cultural Centre at Clonskeagh, 'has set an example of a new type of visit which can serve the process of strengthening inter-faith relations'. Selim alludes to the fact that both first- and second-level education systems present 'challenges and difficulties' for Muslims in Ireland. He has, as might be expected, a special welcome for the creation of a multi-faith school under Jewish, Catholic and Muslim patronage, located in the Catholic diocese of Kildare and Leighlin.

Much indeed will depend on religious leadership in the making of twenty-first century Ireland, but a caveat or two come to mind and a Catholic commentator may be excused for thinking especially of his own Church. The first caveat relates to the risk that the conduct of future dialogue will be left to leaders only. The resulting impoverishment of political life hardly needs stating; 'democratic deficit' isn't just a cliché of the politics of the European Union.

The impoverishment of a Catholic contribution is no less certain and no less deplorable in its results. Conversation within the Irish Catholic Church, at the level of the parish and the diocese, between people and priest, priest and bishop, perhaps bishop and bishops' Conference, improved as it is in some matters and in some places, does not yet adequately reflect the fact that 'the Church' isn't just the hierarchy or the clergy but a community of the baptised, called together in the faith that Jesus Christ is Lord.

A second caveat is of a different order. The Catholic community in Ireland is at present receiving much-needed encouragement, not just from the presence of immigrants who profess and practice their Christian faith with an exemplary seriousness, but from the presence among us also of immigrants of other faiths, especially those whose faith is in Allah. It is something of an understandable relief to the religiously observant that the limitations of European-type secularisms are disclosing themselves as it were unbidden, in such diverse settings as Turkey and France.

However, if all that ensues from this is that church leaders get their wind back, so to say, in a way that risks turning confidence into arrogance and that induces blindness to the variety of *all* the signs of the times, the Christian gospel will assuredly not be served. In our country the decline in church attendance and related phenomena cannot just be put down to bad faith on the part of 'the Pope's children'. Irish secularism may not be noted for its intellectual content but that doesn't mean that it has none. A conversation about Ireland's future that is inclusive must engage the minds and hearts of our secularists too.

NOTES
1   The text of the Archbishop's lecture is found at the BBC News website. Accessed 27 July 2008.

9.
No Catholic Need Apply?

Commentators are fond of quoting de Tocqueville's remark that on his arrival in America what struck him first was the pervasiveness of religion. A visitor from Europe today is not less likely to be impressed, though, of course, for different reasons, especially if the visit takes place in the year of a presidential election. Polls have reported that over 60 per cent of the electorate want the President of the United States to be 'religious'. From early in their campaigns, the candidates in 2008 didn't hesitate to demonstrate their religious credentials, and the subject of religion was rarely out of media during the entire campaign.

The requisite credentials are various: membership of a church, prayer and church attendance, and support for what have come to be called faith initiatives in spheres such as education and the social services. However, it soon becomes apparent that what is critical is a candidate's view on a number of issues that are usually described as religious: same-sex unions, embryonic stem-cell research, euthanasia and especially abortion.

These may strike the reader as more exactly described as moral issues, as indeed they are. Even secular commentary has a tendency to identify morality and religion, especially when, as in this case, a concern with the issues is associated in the public mind with Catholics and Evangelical Christians. The association is understandable, for Catholics and Evangelicals are at one in questioning their morality and leaders of both groups have been vocal in opposing them. However, to describe them as religious can be misleading, in that opposition may then be represented as 'sectarian' and hence out of place in a modern secular society. The fact that mainline Christian teaching about them is characteristically defended on rational grounds does little to dispel the impression that what Catholics hold is a matter of 'faith' and not of reason.

Catholic teaching on abortion in particular, it soon becomes clear too, presents a special problem for a Catholic candidate for office. Abortion is a lawful option under the US Constitution and, as the law stands, it would be unconstitutional to abridge what has come to be called a woman's right to choose. A Catholic president – or senator, representative, governor or judge – must seem compelled to complicity in what church teaching holds to be immoral. Should candidates indicate an interest in changing the law, their electoral prospects may be imperilled, given a fairly general support for the law as it stands.

A FATEFUL CASE

The law stands as it is because of a decision of the US Supreme Court in 1973 in a case called *Roe v Wade*, when it struck down as unconstitutional any law in every state that curtailed the right of a woman to choose to have an abortion. A reversal of this finding is commonly taken to be a *sine qua non* by those who hold that life from conception is entitled to the law's protection. Reversal must be by majority decision of the nine-member Supreme Court, which means that it would need at least five justices in favour. Appointments to the bench of the Supreme Court are, therefore, seen as critical to the outcome of the abortion controversy.

Justices of the Supreme Court are appointed by the President, albeit that nominees run the gauntlet of Congressional hearings as to their fitness, so it is inevitable that a presidential election should generate special interest among abortion campaigners pro and con. In the 2008 campaign, interest on this score was heightened, both because fresh appointments to the bench were due before long and because four of the current justices were Catholics, it being taken for granted in much commentary that a Catholic – or at any rate a Republican – appointee must tip the balance in favour of a reversal of *Roe*. The implications of that assumption for the professionalism of the judges or the integrity of constitutional jurisprudence didn't seem to trouble enthusiasts for change.

All of this is background to a presidential contest in which the Republican candidate John McCain declared that his would be a 'pro-life' presidency, while the Democratic vice-presidential candidate Joe Biden is well known to be a practising Catholic. Add to this that Senator McCain was a supporter of the war in Iraq and that his rival Barack Obama opposed it from the start. The complexities are rife for exploiting, but in any case there's enough in the mix to give rise to some confusion as to what a Catholic voter is expected to make of it all.

'FAITHFUL CITIZENSHIP'
What Catholics are expected to make of their civic responsibilities was the subject of a teaching document issued earlier in the campaign by the Conference of Catholic Bishops, in line with a practice initiated some decades ago. The document draws on past statements of the Conference and on Catholic teaching generally, in a comprehensive account of the principles that come in play when Catholics seek to discharge their civic responsibilities in the light of a Christian vision of life. That vision summons Catholics to take part in politics as a matter of moral obligation, in a time of political challenges that call for 'urgent moral choices'.

In the Conference's statement the choices and challenges are elaborated systematically and the makings of a Catholic response is sketched. The statement's starting-point is a sombre picture of life in the US today:

> a nation at war, with all of its human costs; a country often divided by race and ethnicity; a nation of immigrants struggling with immigration ... an affluent society where too many live in poverty; part of a global community confronting terrorism and facing urgent threats to our environment; a culture built on families, where some now question the value of marriage and family life ... We pride ourselves on supporting human rights; but we fail even to protect the fundamental right to life, especially for unborn children.[1]

'A CONSISTENT ETHIC OF LIFE'

A Catholic's engagement in politics is meant to be guided by what the bishops call a consistent ethic of life, and they enjoin Catholic voters to use Catholic teaching in evaluating candidates' positions. Citing an earlier Conference document, they call on voters 'to see beyond party politics, to analyse campaign rhetoric critically and to choose their political leaders according to principle, not party affiliation or mere self-interest'.[2] It is not their intention to tell Catholics how to vote, the bishops say, but rather to help them form their consciences properly, the better to carry out their responsibilities to the political process.

Even this much makes it plain that the moral canvas envisaged by the bishops is variegated and broad, nor does anything in its elaboration give ground for the charge that their view of politics is 'single issue'. Indeed the statement expressly repudiates this charge more than once: 'As Catholics we are not single issue voters'; and a Catholic political ethic 'neither treats all issues as

morally equivalent nor reduces Catholic teaching to one
or two issues'. Rather 'it anchors the Catholic
commitment to defend human life and other human
rights, from conception until natural death, in the
fundamental obligation to respect the dignity of every
human being as a child of God'.

In setting out the demands of this ethic, the statement
proposes some unvarying moral principles: respect for life,
for example, and the prohibition of every direct attack on
innocent human life; regard for justice and opposition to
any violation of basic human rights; a commitment to the
common good and rejection of all merely sectional
interest. However, the statement recognises that there is
a difference between principle and practical
implementation and it acknowledges that there may be
room for difference of opinion as to the best way to secure
moral values in practice.

'PRUDENTIAL JUDGEMENT'
This should not lead, however, to an easy acquiescence
in laws that are morally flawed, the bishops insist. On the
contrary, 'those who formulate legislation have an
obligation in conscience to work towards correcting
morally defective laws, lest they be guilty of cooperating
in evil and sinning against the common good'. In such a
situation, 'prudential judgement is needed to determine
how to do what is possible to restore justice – even if
partially or gradually – without ever abandoning a moral
commitment to the full protection of life from conception
to natural death'.[3]

Prudential judgement is a concept familiar in
Catholic moral theology, with roots in the thought of
Aquinas and ultimately in the ethics of Aristotle. *The
Catechism of the Catholic Church*, as the bishops
recall, defines prudence as the virtue that enables us
'to discern our true good in every circumstance and to

choose the right means of achieving it' (CCC 1806); and
the statement goes on to elaborate: 'Prudence shapes
and informs our ability to deliberate over available
alternatives, to determine what is most fitting to a
specific context, and to act.' The bishops grant that
'Catholics may choose different ways to respond to
social problems', even as they insist that there can be
no differing about 'the obligation to protect human life
and dignity and help build through moral means a more
just and peaceful world'.

Some critics complain that what the bishops want is to
impose a Catholic ethic by way of the law of the land;
something thought especially out of place in a country
whose Constitution guarantees freedom of religious belief
and practice, a guarantee that is called for by Catholic
teaching itself. Catholic teaching does indeed affirm a right
to religious liberty; but that right's exercise, like the exercise
of any right, is constrained by the claims of the common
good.[4] The common good in a Catholic view includes a right
to life 'from conception to natural death', a right that is
everyone's in virtue of human dignity and that the teaching
defends on rational as well as faith grounds.

In this view it is wrong to describe opposition to
abortion as a matter of 'private morality', a matter of
personal conscience judgement that is not for
enforcement by legislation. This is the basis for
Catholic criticism of the position adopted by Senator
Kerry in 2004, as in 1984 by Congresswoman Geraldine
Ferraro and in the 2008 campaign by Senator Biden and
House Speaker Nancy Pelosi, when they invoked a
distinction between personal conviction and public
responsibility to the Constitution as a basis for their
unwillingness to challenge the legal status quo. It is
also the ground on which the Democratic party is
faulted insofar as it has declined to promote reform of
abortion law.

MAY A CATHOLIC APPLY?

Does it follow that a Catholic is in conscience precluded from seeking office unless he or she is going to work for a change in the law? In practice, this would probably mean that a Catholic couldn't run for a Democratic nomination or at any rate that a Catholic Democrat had but a slim chance at the polls. Or does it follow that a Catholic citizen could not in conscience vote for Barack Obama, who had declared himself in favour of the finding in *Roe v Wade*? It might seem that the answer is obvious: such self-denying ordinances seem contrary to plain common sense. Yet each has been seriously put forward and not just by religious fanatics or partisan manipulators of truth.

So, for example, in a book which appeared in the course of the campaign,[5] Archbishop of Denver Charles J. Chaput reports a question he was asked by a friend: could a Catholic vote in good conscience for a candidate who is pro-choice? 'The answer is *I* couldn't,' is how Archbishop Chaput replies (his italic), and he glosses his reply in brief: 'Supporting a "right" to choose abortion simply masks and evades what abortion really is: the deliberate killing of innocent life. I know nothing that can morally offset that kind of evil.'

Contrast this with the stance of Douglas Kmiec, an academic lawyer who has taught at Notre Dame and the Catholic University of America, in a book also published during the campaign.[6] Kmiec endorsed the candidature of Senator Obama notwithstanding that the latter had declared in favour of *Roe*'s affirmation of a right to choose, because he believes that Obama's policy – to try to remedy the conditions which drive many women to abortion – is more likely to lead to a reduction in the number of abortions, which he sees as the true pro-life task. To hope for a reversal of *Roe* is in Kmiec's view to place trust in a case that is not yet filed or argued, in the expectation that a pro-life president must pack the bench so as to ensure a favourable outcome.

Kmiec's view of the pro-life task is a widely respected one, for not only is he an academic lawyer who believes that *Roe v Wade* was wrongly decided, but for almost four decades he has been an activist in the Catholic pro-life movement. He is also a life-long Republican, on the conservative side of the party by his own profession and by common consent. He was not surprised, he says, by the consternation that his endorsement of Obama provoked among Republicans, but he didn't anticipate the depth of the reaction among Catholics, least of all that he would be refused Holy Communion.

SO WHO IS RIGHT?

On the whole, Archbishop Chaput's book is a clear and fair account of Catholic teaching about the values of life, and about the political responsibilities which adherence to that teaching brings. After declaring that he himself could not in conscience vote for a pro-choice candidate he adds immediately that he knows Catholics who can – 'sincere Catholics who reason differently' and who are 'deeply troubled by war and other serious injustices'. His view of them? 'I respect them. I don't agree with their calculus.'

Archbishop Chaput doesn't think that their decision can be easily reached. 'What distinguishes such voters … is that they put real effort into struggling with the abortion issue. They don't vote reflexively for the candidate of "their" party. They don't accept abortion as a closed matter. They refuse to stop pushing to change the direction of their party on the abortion issue. They won't be quiet. They keep fighting for a more humane party platform – one that would vow to protect the unborn child. Their decision to vote for a "pro-choice" candidate is genuinely painful and never easy for them.'

A reader of Kmiec's book will agree that this is an apt description of his position. However, Chaput hits upon the nub of the difference between them, namely the calculus that each employs in deciding for whom he should vote.

Calculus is a word that may evoke unease in someone who repudiates what is called consequentialism in moral judgement; who believes, that is, that actions may be wrong in themselves, no matter that they may have good results. The view that it is always wrong to end wilfully the life of a human being, 'from conception to natural death', is an example of such a belief. It might seem, therefore, that any use of a calculus, a balancing of pros and cons, can have no place in the moral judgement of a Catholic.

However, in Catholic teaching, a calculation of pros and cons can sometimes legitimately arise, as it does, for example, in medical ethics when there is question of discontinuing 'extraordinary' treatment that is not going to make a patient better. It arises also in standard textbook accounts of the morality of cooperating in the wrong-doing of another, which is, from a Catholic point of view, what is at stake in the legalisation of abortion. Standard teaching is that provided one doesn't oneself want to bring about the evil that a wrongdoer wants to accomplish, and that one's cooperation is neither immediate nor proximate, it will be permissible to cooperate if one has a good enough reason. In the language of the textbooks this is expressed by saying that *formal* cooperation is never justified, but *material* cooperation may be justified if it is sufficiently remote and if there is a *proportionate* reason.[7]

It is obvious that the application of these principles in a practical case can never be trouble free. One might agree, as do most protagonists – including (it seems) Chaput and (certainly) Kmiec – that the question at issue in the 2008 presidential election was one of material rather than formal cooperation. But how do you decide whether cooperation is proximate or remote, and how do you decide what counts as proportionate? Is it remote or proximate cooperation if a lawmaker or judge goes along with the law that lets women choose abortion? Then, of course, there's the question what it means to 'go along with'. And if proportionality means (roughly) that the good that is hoped for must outweigh the evil entailed, how do you evaluate this?

Archbishop Chaput and Professor Kmiec come to different conclusions even though they share all relevant essential beliefs. Some find such differences hard to understand, disturbing even; and some disingenuously attribute them to a failure of intellectual rigour, questionable motivations or an outright lack of good faith. Yet uncertainty about what exactly to do in practice, and the validity sometimes of alternative applications of a general principle, are not unfamiliar in our everyday moral experience, familiar enough to escape our conscious reflection.

You could acknowledge, for example, that it is a Christian's duty to help people who are in need and yet not think it right to give money to people who ask for it in the street. Christian morality requires that Ireland share its wealth with countries that are less well off, but Christians differ as to whether this is done better through non-governmental rather than governmental agencies. Or one might encounter a dilemma, great or small. Should we tell the truth if telling it will break a confidence? Are we obliged to keep a promise, solemnly made in the best of faith, when it turns out later that to do so will bring us harm? Are we to blow the whistle on a co-worker's dishonesty if our doing so will cause his family to be put in want? Is it right to give a loan to a hard-up neighbour when we know that a lot of his money goes on drink?

Uncertainty and difference of opinion about matters such as these merely illustrate an observation of

Aquinas: 'The more you descend into detail the more it appears how the general rule admits of exceptions, so that you have to hedge it with cautions and qualifications.'[8] The US controversy illustrates also another insight of St Thomas, when he likens the task of the lawmaker to that of a practitioner of one of the arts; as when an architect 'determines that a house should be in this or that style';[9] the point being that there can be more than one way of translating a moral insight into law, and room for debate about how best it should be done.

SLOGAN WARS

The political philosopher Amy Gutmann has written of the lure of extremist rhetoric in democratic controversy and what she says is all too relevant to debates involving religion and politics.

> Part of the lure lies in the fact that it is easier to believe passionately in a value or cause without regard to subtlety, reasoned argument, probabilistic evidence and vigorously tested scientific theory or fact. Expressions of single-minded visions for solving problems and changing society can make complexity and uncertainty, frustration and regret, all appear to evaporate. Another part of the lure is that having comrades-in-argument is comforting.[10]

Single-mindedness has a place sometimes, as Gutmann indeed concedes, and comradeship in a cause is natural. However, single-mindedness may turn to fanaticism, comradeship become a closing of the ranks against anyone who thinks differently from oneself. 'Slogan' is from the Irish and Scots Gaelic *slua-ghairm*, meaning war-cry – literally the shout of a crowd. A crowd's shout or a war-cry are not the language of persuasion and pacific argument, in John Courtney Murray's phrase. Gutmann names the dangers: 'Mobilising one's base and arousing people's passions are natural parts of democratic politics ... The problem with extremist rhetoric is that it mobilises the base by spurning reason and playing exclusively to the antagonistic passions of disrespect and degradation of argumentative adversaries.'[11]

It is unfortunate that people as morally and religiously serious as Senator Biden and Speaker Pelosi, when asked how they relate their beliefs and their political practice, could do no better than provide an ill-thought-out conception of the difference between public and private morality. It is unfortunate also that a number of individual bishops insisted that a Catholic in good conscience could not vote for the Democratic ticket. The religious tradition from which the bishops and the politicians come is a sophisticated one and, as the Conference statements illustrate, and in a different way the testimony of Douglas Kmiec, it can furnish all that is needed for an account of their task which is not the less visionary for being realistic.

NOTES

1   *Forming Consciences for Faithful Citizenship: A Call to Political Responsibility by the Catholic Bishops of the United States*. All quotations here are from the official summary, the text of which is available – as is the full statement – on the Conference's website at www.usccb.org (last accessed 15 April 2009).

2   *Living the Gospel of Life: A Challenge to American Catholics* (1998), (last accessed 16 October 2008).

3   This echoes the Conference's *Catholics in Political Life* (2004) and *Living the Gospel of Life* (1998). The bishops' teaching in these matters is grounded in *Evangelium vitae* (1993), an encyclical letter of Pope John Paul II (see especially par. 73), and in a Doctrinal Note on the Participation of Catholics in Political Life (2002) from the Congregation for the Doctrine of the Faith. Vatican (including papal) documents are accessible at www.vatican.va.

4   Vatican Council II, *Dignitatis humanae*: see especially pars 2 and 6.

5   *Render Unto Caesar*, New York, London, Toronto, Sydney, Auckland, 2008. Quotations are from p. 229.

6   *Can a Catholic Support Him? Asking the Big Question about Barack Obama*, Woodstock and New York, 2008.

7   Proportionate reason has had its own problems during the past few decades despite its excellent pedigree in the thought of St Thomas Aquinas; cf John Paul II's encyclical *Veritatis splendor* which criticises 'proportionalists'. It should be noted that it's not the concept itself that is criticised but the notion that it can be used to resolve all moral dilemmas, a position taken to imply that there is no act which is 'intrinsically evil'.

8   *Summa theologiae*, 1a 2ae, 94,4. Translation as in the Blackfriars edition, vol. 28.

9   Ibid., 95,2. See chapter 10.

10 Amy Gutmann, 'The Lure and Dangers of Extremist Rhetoric', *Daedalus*, Fall 2007, p. 71.

11 Ibid., p. 72

10.
Aquinas,
Morality and Law

At the beginning of his book Law, *Liberty and Morality*, H.L.A. Hart lists four questions that may be asked about the relationship between morality and law. The first is whether the development of law has been influenced by morality and vice versa. The second is whether an adequate definition of law must contain some reference to morality. The third asks whether and how the law may be open to moral criticism. The fourth has to do with the legal enforcement of morals: the question whether the law should restrain immorality, that is, whether what is immoral should be a crime.[1]

All these questions have received attention from legal and political philosophers during the past several centuries, but in recent decades there has been particular discussion of the fourth. Professor Hart's book was a reply to Sir Patrick (later Lord) Devlin's famous Maccabean lecture on the legal enforcement of morals, which was itself a response to the view adopted in the Wolfenden Report on Homosexual Offences and Prostitution.[2] Their exchanges, which paralleled remarkably a nineteenth century debate between John Stuart Mill and James Fitzjames Stephen, have been the subject of much writing in the fields of political philosophy and jurisprudence.[3]

Debates about the enforcement of morals have also been prominent in public discussion in this country in recent decades, as our laws on divorce, homosexual behaviour, abortion and the sale of contraceptives have come in for scrutiny. Nor is Ireland the only place in which the issues are alive: in the past year or so Britain has seen yet another debate concerning its abortion laws; and in the United States, abortion law is latterly joined by same-sex marriage as a focus for continuing public discussion of the interrelationships of morality, religion and the law.

In the context of these debates it is interesting to look again at what the masters of Christian tradition made of some of the issues. It is especially interesting to look at the thought of St Thomas Aquinas. As he did in so many other areas, he both summed up a tradition and gave it a personal stamp. His writing on law and politics has been influential. It is, of course, anachronistic to seek in St Thomas the answers – or even all the questions – that are appropriate to our times. Yet it remains instructive to observe the way in which one of the chief moulders of Christian thinking handled questions about law and morals as they were posed in his time and place.

St Thomas' treatment of law is to be found in its most sustained and comprehensive form in Questions 90–97 of the first Part of the Second Book of the *Summa theologiae*[4], often therefore called his 'tract' or 'treatise' on law. Of course, for a full account we would need to examine other passages in the *Summa*, as well as some of his other writings. And it has to be remembered that the treatise on law belongs in a wider theological design. But for our purposes it will suffice to concentrate on the account found in Questions 90–97.

A preliminary point concerns Thomas' methodology, which was the methodology of the philosophers and theologians of medieval times. The material treated was set out in 'Questions' and these were subdivided into 'Articles'. The heading of each Article was itself in the form of a question, and the response began by positing and defending a point of view opposed to the author's own. This was followed by the *corpus* or body of the Article, in which the thought of the author himself was elaborated. The Article ended with a reply to each of the arguments adduced at the start in favour of the alternative view.

Thomas begins his treatise with an enquiry into the nature, kinds and effects of law in general. These are the subjects of Questions 90, 91 and 92 respectively. Next he takes up for a closer examination each of the main kinds of law – the Eternal Law, the Natural Law and Human Law. The first of these is dealt with in Question 93, the second in Question 94, while human law is treated over the three Questions 95 to 97.

From the outset Thomas offers an appraisal of law that is positive, referring to it as one of the ways in which God 'builds us up' in virtue. This is a significant break with a contemporary view, derived ultimately from St Augustine (who in so many ways was Aquinas' source and authority), according to which law exists *propter peccatum*, i.e. as a coercive curb on the waywardness of sinful human beings. Thomas' relative optimism emerges again in the final Article of Question 92, which asks whether making people good is one of the effects of law. The core of the answer is yes, though, as we shall see, this is later importantly qualified in respect of human (as distinct from divine) law.

Human or man-made law is first mentioned in Question 91, in which St Thomas considers the various kinds of law. He has already established the existence of an *Eternal Law* whereby 'the whole community of the universe is governed by God's mind';[5] and of a *Natural Law*, which he sees as 'a sharing in the Eternal Law by intelligent creatures'.[6] In the fashion of scholastic methodology he posits first the pointlessness of a purported 'human law': 'Natural law, it has been stated, is a sharing in the Eternal Law, through which, as Augustine remarks, all things are consummately ordered. Therefore natural law suffices for the ordering of human affairs and any human law is needless.'[7]

It is for an answer to this objection in particular that the *corpus* of the article prepares the way. It begins by adverting to a distinction between the theoretical and practical reason, and to an analogy between their respective operations.

> As we have seen, law is a kind of dictate of the practical reason. The processes of the theoretic and practical reasons are parallel; both, we have held, start from certain principles and come to certain conclusions. Accordingly we say this, that just as from indemonstrable principles that are instinctively recognised the theoretic reason draws the conclusions of the various sciences not imparted by nature but discovered by reasoned effort, so also from natural law precepts as from common and indemonstrable principles the human reason comes down to making more specific arrangements. Now these particular arrangements human reason arrives at are called 'human laws', provided they fulfil the essential conditions of law already indicated.[8]

These 'essential conditions' are those incorporated in the celebrated definition of law as 'an ordinance of reason for the common good, [enacted] by him who has care of the community, and promulgated'.[9]

In the light of all this, Aquinas answers his own objection as follows:

> The human reason cannot fully grasp the meaning of God's command, but it partially holds it after its own fashion. The consequence is that just as the theoretic reason by its nature partakes of divine

wisdom, and therefore we have from within an awareness of certain general principles, though not that proper knowledge of every single truth which divine wisdom comprehends, so on the part of practical reason we enter into the Eternal Law according to some general principles without knowing all individual directives, though these are comprehended in the Eternal Law. Hence the need for human reason to proceed further and sanction particular enactments of law.[10]

I have quoted at length from this article because it sets out the essentials of Aquinas' view of the nature and significance of human law, and it reveals the spirit of his approach. A link with God's eternal design is established, as is a relationship with natural law. The positive note already sounded in the introduction is sounded again, and the basis for Thomas' optimism is revealed. Thus the ground is prepared for the detailed examination of human law that occupies Questions 95, 96 and 97.

These Questions deal respectively with human law 'in itself', the power of human law, and law and change. Some of the material is technical, arising out of some characteristic preoccupations of the canonists and jurists of medieval times. However, Aquinas canvasses also some themes that concern us as much as they did him. The first is one already signalled in the passage just quoted from Question 91, the relationship between human law and natural law. The question put is whether every man-made law is derived from natural law. Aquinas' answer is in essence yes; but the precise meaning of this affirmation is important and the detail of his argument requires attention.

One must first notice the exalted place which Thomas gives the natural law. It is a sharing of the divine law on the part of rational creatures;[11] and in the body of Article 2 of Question 91 the import of this has been indicated: 'Among [beings] intelligent creatures are ranked under divine Providence the more nobly because they take part in Providence by their providing for themselves and others.'[12] In Aquinas' vision all things move towards their own 'ends', the purposes for which they exist, and the human being does so rationally. The human role is, therefore, constructive or creative; the human person, under God, has to make something of him/herself and of the world.

Notice also his exalted view of even man-made law. Having established the existence of an Eternal Law whereby 'the whole community of the universe is governed by God's mind',[13] and of a Natural Law which is a 'sharing in the Eternal Law by rational creatures',[14] he sees the lawmaker's task as one of reasoning from Natural Law's principles to certain 'more specific arrangements' – called human 'laws' inasmuch as they 'fulfil the essential conditions of law already indicated'[15]. These conditions have been set out, as we have seen in his examination of the nature of law: it is an ordinance of reason, in aid of the common good, by whomever has charge of the community, and promulgated.[16]

Here then, to recapitulate, is a view of human law that links it not just with the moral law but with God's design for the whole creation. In that design each creature has its purpose, each moves towards its own goal. 'Among [beings] intelligent creatures are ranked under divine Providence the more nobly because they take part in Providence by their providing for themselves and others.'[17] The human creature's goal is God, towards whom we move, drawn by grace, yet freely. The human role is creative; men and women, under God, are called to make something of themselves and of their world, discovering and respecting the divine design.

In Aquinas' perspective, therefore, the making of law is in service of virtue, and law is derived from morality in two ways. First, it may be deduced, as a conclusion is deduced from a premise: for instance, 'You must not commit murder' can be inferred from 'You must do harm to nobody'. Second, a law may represent one of a number of alternative options towards ensuring what we might call the realisation of a moral insight. So, for example, morality requires that crime be punished. However, it is for the lawmaker to choose the form that a punishment should take.[18]

This is important, because it shows that though law in Thomas' mind translates a moral viewpoint, it is not always as by direct and necessary inference. Another way of putting this is to say that a particular law, though it embodies a moral insight, may not be the only way in which the insight can be made concrete. So in modern terms we should say that there is room for debate about the appropriateness of any particular item of lawmaking.

Important too, and instructive, are the parallels that Thomas draws in the case of each kind of legislation: 'The first process [deduction] is like that of the sciences where inferences are demonstratively drawn from principles. The second process is like that of the arts, where a special shape is given to a general idea, as when an architect determines that a house should be in this or that style.'[19]

There is, therefore, an *art* of lawmaking and it is not the same as the art of the moralist; and its autonomy must be respected. This autonomy does not bespeak indifference to morality: we have seen that both kinds of lawmaking render, even if in each case differently, an essentially moral insight. The legislator must respect the moral order, and may not make a law that undermines or contravenes it. Indeed, Thomas says that a lawmaker's command has the force of law to the extent that it is just;

and 'if on any head it is at variance with natural law, it will not be law but a corruption of law'.[20] Yet law and politics have their own autonomy. In pursuit of their purposes they have their own art and it is not for the moralist to instruct the legislator on the art of legislation.

This leads naturally to a closer examination of Aquinas' teaching on the 'enforcement' of morality by the law. We might recall that in Question 92, when discussing the effects of law, he stated that it was a function of law to make people good. At that point he was discussing law in general, including the Eternal Law and the Natural Law, and he was not yet interested in the specific role of human positive law. As far as human law is concerned, the sense of the reply at that point is, as Gilby puts it, that the keeping of a just law makes people worthy with respect to what it covers, not that it makes them wholly good.[21] According to the *Summa contra Gentiles*,[22] making people wholly good is an effect only of God's law; and many passages in the *Summa Theologiae* make it plain that it is accomplished through the divine gift of charity.[23]

So what, practically, can be expected, or what ought to be sought, from human law as regards morality? This is first considered in a general way when Thomas asks about the utility of man-made law. Each human being has an 'innate bent' for virtue, yet 'to come to its fulness' we need education.[24]

> Now for the young apt for deeds of virtue by good natural disposition or by custom or, better still, by divine gift, all that is required is the fatherly discipline of admonition. Not all the young, however, are like that; some are bumptious, headlong in vice, not amenable to advice, and these have to be held back from evil by fear and force, so that they at least stop doing mischief and leave others in peace. Becoming

so habituated they may come to do of their own
accord what earlier they did from fear, and grow
virtuous. This schooling through the pressure
exerted through the fear of punishment is the
discipline of human law.[25]

In articles 2 and 3 of Question 96 he asks in turn whether
it is the business of law to restrain all vice or to enforce
every virtue. It will be convenient here if we take the
second question first.

We have seen, says Thomas, that law is ordained to
the common good and, in principle, there is no virtue of
which some activity cannot be enjoined by law.
'Nevertheless, human law does not enjoin every act of
every virtue, but those acts only which serve the
common good, either immediately, as when the social
order is directly involved from the nature of things, or
mediately, as when measures of good discipline are
passed by the legislator to train citizens to maintain
justice and peace in the community.'[26]

So the virtuous acts enjoined by law are those only
which directly or indirectly concern the common good
and the social order. Moreover, Aquinas is well aware
that virtue as such cannot be produced by a law, as is
clear from his reply to the second objection.

One may speak of an act of virtue in two senses.
First, to refer to the deed of virtue, thus, for
instance, the fair dealing in which justice is engaged,
or the brave action in which courage is engaged: this
is what the law prescribes for those acts of virtue it
deals with. Secondly, to refer to its being done in the
virtuous style of a good man: as such it always
springs from virtue, and does not fall under the
precept of the law, but is the end to which the
lawgiver intends the law to lead.[27]

This alludes to a key difference between morality and law: that morality is concerned with such 'interior' factors as disposition, attitude, motivation and intention, while law normally is not.[28] The point here is that only external performance can be imposed by law; one may be compelled to pay a debt, but out of fear rather than from a sense of justice.

If the law cannot enforce virtue, should it try to restrain every vice? The core of the answer is no, but the detail of the argument is again revealing.

Article 2 begins with an objection based upon a dictum of Isidore of Seville: 'Laws are made in order that their threat shall repress effrontery.' Thomas observes that such repression would be ineffective unless law restrained all moral evil: 'Therefore human law ought to restrain them all.' The second and third objections arise from positions that he himself has already adopted:

> (2) Moreover, it has been stated that the lawgiver's intention is to make citizens virtuous. A man, however, cannot be virtuous unless he keeps off vice of every kind. Hence it is for human law to rule out all vices.
> (3) Furthermore, it has been stated that human law is derived from natural law. Yet all the vices conflict with natural law. Therefore human law should hold them down.[29]

He invokes the authority of Augustine for the contrary view and he proceeds to make the case as follows:

> As we have seen, law is established as a kind of rule or measure for human acts. Now, as noted in the Metaphysics, a measure ought to be of the same kind as the thing it measures; different things have different standards. Hence law should be appointed

to men according to their condition; Isidore remarks how law should 'be possible according both to nature and the custom of the country'.[30]

There is, therefore, a criterion of practicability; the lawmaker must have regard to the capacity of his subjects.

> The ability and resource for acting in a certain way spring from an interior disposition or habit; the same course of action is not possible for a man who has a habit of virtue and for a man who lacks it, nor for a grown-up and a child: this is why the same laws do not apply, for many things are allowed in the young for which older people are punished, or at least blamed. Likewise many things may be let pass in people of mediocre morals which cannot be countenanced in their betters.[31]

The fact is that 'law is laid down for a great number of people, of which the majority have no high standard of morality'.

> Therefore it does not forbid all the vices, from which the upright can keep away, but only those grave ones which the average man can avoid, and chiefly those which do harm to others and have to be stopped if human society is to be maintained, such as murder and theft, and so forth.[32]

In this argument the notion of law as educative is maintained but there is a realism about its potential. Aquinas accepts as a fact that the majority of people 'have no high standard of morality' and considers that the law must accommodate to that fact. The reply to the second objection clarifies the point: the purpose of the law is to bring people to virtue 'not suddenly but step by step'. 'Therefore it does not all at once burden the crowd of imperfect men with the responsibilities assumed by men of the highest character, nor require them to keep away from all evils, lest, not sturdy enough to bear the strain, they break out into greater wrongs.'[33]

Thomas' stance here is far from a modern recognition of 'pluralism' of moral value: for him, differences of moral belief and performance are rooted in waywardness, or at best in ignorance, and the law's accommodations are necessitated by regrettable practical necessity. However, while it would be wrong to insinuate that his standpoint is anything like that of a modern, the tenor and spirit of his treatment are instructive for us. It is well to be aware that at the heart of the Christian tradition of theologising about law, there was considerable subtlety, founded in a sense of the practical and the humane.

NOTES

1   H.L.A. Hart, Law, *Liberty and Morality*, Oxford University Press, 1968, pp. 1–4.
2   Patrick Devlin, 'Morals and the Criminal Law', in *The Enforcement of Morals*, Oxford University Press, 1965, p. 1ff.
3   Both Hart's and Devlin's books contain select bibliography. Additional bibliography may be found in standard introductions to Anglo-American jurisprudence and legal philosophy.
4   Text and translation here is from the Blackfriars Edition, vol. 28, edited by Thomas Gilby OP (Blackfriars, 1966); hereinafter cited as Bl, followed by the page number.
5   Q. 91, art. 1. Bl 19.
6   Q. 91, art. 2. Bl 23.
7   Q. 91, art. 3. Bl 25.
8   Ibid. Here and throughout the treatise Aquinas makes use of the thought of Aristotle.
9   Q. 90, arts. 1–4.
10 Q. 91, art. 3, ad 1. Bl 27.
11 Q, 91, art. 2. Bl 22. cf. ad 3 (Bl 24).
12 Ibid.
13 Q. 91, art. 1. Bl 19.
14 Q. 91, art. 2. Bl 23.

15 Q. 91, art. 3. BI 27.
16 Q. 90, arts. 1–4. BI 2–17. cf. also Q. 95, art. 3.
17 Q. 91, art. 2. BI 23.
18 Q. 95, art. 2. BI 107. The examples are Aquinas' .
19 Q. 95 art. 2. BI 105, 107. Gilby translates '*determinatio*' as 'constructional implementation', intending to bring out the point that 'art adds something of its own to this process of making determinate'. He remarks, 'This is a key passage in the history of State theory, and an early recognition by a social philosopher that pure legality and politics have their own proper interests which cannot be explicated in terms of individual and social morality' (BI 105, note c).
20 Q. 95, art. 2. BI 105. cf. Q. 93, art. 4, ad 2. (BI 61).
21 BI 41, note *b*.
22 SCG III, 115-117
23 E.g. 1a 2ae Q. 65, arts. 1 & 2; 2a 2ae, Q. 23, art. 8, Q. 47, arts. 6 & 7.
24 Q. 95, art. 1. BI 101.
25 Ibid.
26 Q. 96, art. 3. BI 127
27 Ad 2. loc. cit.
28 An exception is the criminal law's interest in *mens rea*.
29 BI 123.
30 Ibid.
31 Ibid.
32 Ibid.
33 BI 125.

11.
'Wragg is in Custody':
A Court Case Observed

The front of the Old Bailey is being repaired and scaffolding rises from the street to the roof. From a certain vantage point there is an illusion that the goddess Justice is standing on the scaffold. Of course, they would have to take away the scales. And her sword.

You cross the street to the new entrance and a little further down there is a window in which may be read notices of the daily business of each court. On 2 November 1987 one notice tells of a challenge to the Crown by Hugh Callaghan, Patrick Hill, Gerard Hunter, Richard McIlkenny, William Power and John Walker. Their case will be heard in Court 12 by Lord Chief Justice Lane and Lords Justices O'Connor and Stephen Brown. The notice is not removed until late in the afternoon of 9 December.

DAY ONE

There is an excitement outside the court on this bright November Monday. These men are saying that their conviction, twelve years before, on twenty-one counts each of murder, was wrong and should even now be set aside. Today's event is the end of a long haul for them and their relatives and supporters. They have been trying since then to get a fresh hearing for their story. Their story, if accepted, is an indictment of a system whose *raison d'être* is justice.

The men's story and the system's response are going to be observed closely. Hence the reporters and the cameras and the other paraphernalia of media scrutiny. Hence too the senator from Massachusetts, the bishop from Ireland, the Greek lawyer from Amnesty International and others to be known for the moment as 'distinguished observers'. And, of course, the relatives: not unused now, many of them, to the public stare; still, today, hesitant, unsure of who their friends are, timid in the midst of the bustle. Even now, though, it is possible to guess which will assume a public role.

Security is tight and, of course, there are 'incidents'. Everyone is edgy. The police 'have a job to do' – some people are naturally awkward customers. In general, the distinguished observers are treated with somewhat more grace than are others. Later in the hearing there will be instances of inexcusable bureaucratics, as when John Walker's children, over from Derry, are refused admittance to the public gallery because they have 'only' their medical cards for identification. No matter that medical cards are accepted for this purpose in that part of the United Kingdom from which they come. Nor that, over and over again, the Walkers are vouched for by people whose trustworthiness has apparently been officially recognised.

'Court rise'; and it does, and the Justices file in, and in due course we may all sit again. Stillness follows. After a short delay the men enter, their entrance breaking the tension but unleashing feelings that only later could be distinguished and named. Everyone spoke of the shock of seeing how they had aged; but there was also a rush of sadness and then a cold fear. Are these murderers, or some of them? How ordinary they look. Perhaps they are: killers of twenty-one people, most of them young, maimers of many more. Or are they innocent? Innocent all the time, and in jail, and their families without them. If they are, will this court free them? Fear turns to anger: there is too much talk about England's record in regard to us; we should not acquiesce in expectation of the worst. If they are innocent they must be freed. Why did it take so long to come to this?

The men's names are called and they are told to rearrange themselves in alphabetical order and to sit. The case for the appellants is outlined. Their conviction has rested upon twin pillars: confessions and forensic evidence. The fresh evidence will show that these two pillars are and have been cracked, incapable for long more now of bearing the weight which has been placed upon them. In addition, consider the way in which the judge directed the jury: he prevented them from thinking for themselves. This court will have no option but to declare the men's conviction 'unsafe and unsatisfactory'. There is indeed an argument for quashing the conviction forthwith and ordering a retrial. However, the judges do not see it that way. Call the first witness.

Even during the opening submissions the judges have made it plain that counsel for the men had better be careful how they go. Soon a question will arise, whether the judges are so biased as to be incapable of an objective determination of the case. This observer tries to keep an open mind. A certain peevishness on the part of judges is traditional; they are always hard on defence lawyers; and where so much is at stake it is inevitable that they will push against the men's case. Even when judicial intervention seems notably protective of crown witnesses the hope persists that this does not betoken prejudice.

Not that it is easy to retain an open mind. When the men's lawyers ask for leave to recall former PC Mrs Lynas, the judges talk it over privately and agree. The Lord Chief Justice, about to make concessions so as to give her time to get back from Birmingham, is heavily sarcastic when he hears that the lawyers – completely reasonably, one would have thought – have ensured that she is already at hand. Much later in the hearing the judges instinctively turn down an objection on the men's behalf to the introduction of a certain piece of evidence; only to realise as the lawyer begins to speak that the objection should have been allowed. Yet it is not until the judgment that this observer is able finally to make up his mind.

TIME PASSES

Day succeeds day and a kind of familiarity grows. Familiarity, of course, with the rest of the Irishry, among whom unexpected bonds are at least for the moment forged. Familiarity with procedures and surroundings, so that one no longer feels footless. A kind of familiarity even, as time passes, with court personnel, especially the policeman and policewoman most usually on the door. These latter are inclined for banter, and what harm? Only, sometimes you feel slightly guilty because they are of the Other Side.

What 'other side'? Not all English people think alike on this case – nor do all the Irish. And anyway an observer has to stay detached.

There grows a familiarity with the men. Now they nod or wave in the direction of the observers' box, as invariably they have done to their relatives and friends in the galleries. The sense of growing familiarity is eerie, for no words are exchanged, but it is real. Occasional intimations of appreciation of one's presence come via the relatives, but it is only at the end, when word comes of a gift of a copy of Mullin's book signed by each of them, that a sense of the depth of their gratitude strikes. I ask one of the wives why? 'Because you're a priest, and you're there always.'

It is easy to get on with the relatives: they are honest, spirited and unsentimentally thankful for support. Nora Power's Cork accent plays tunes against a northern backing. (This observer has more than one culture gap to contend with.) Sometimes one or other of them has enough and disappears for a day, but is back, fighting, soon. Like all decent people they don't always get on with each other, but they get over their differences, absorbed in a common pursuit. They are thankful for interest, but they are also private people and one guesses that they could repel, politely, the intrusive do-gooder. Of which breed there are a few here.

A sense of the men and the relatives is what keeps the observer from straying too far from his task. And it is possible to stray, for honest reasons and bad. I find that I belong to two 'clubs', the lawyers and the priests (I've just remembered something from the New Testament), and it is very easy to lose oneself in whichever happens at a particular time to be convenient. It is, I hope, forgivable; for sometimes the attempt to stay with the task is hard and it is a relief to fall back on unspoken affinities. A sense of belonging to the Irish 'team' is also seductive. More of this later.

So it is possible to stray from the task. A recurrent hazard is of being carried away by the legal game, played superbly by two superb teams of lawyers. For the law is a game. It has rules and skills, and at times a life of its own. It is possible to forget that the rules and skills are in aid of justice, of securing for people what is their due. It is, sometimes, possible to forget that we are in Court 12 to try to discover what was the due of the six men in the dock and their families, with regard also to the due of the dead and maimed of Birmingham and *their* relatives. A chance glance at the gallery or dock brings one back.

Week succeeds week. In retrospect, particular moments are beginning to stand out. Mrs Lynas' second appearance, of course: dramatic, tense, entirely believable. The opening of the Crown forensic expert Frank Skuse's cross-examination by Michael Mansfield, in which in the first minute he is caught in a lie. A sudden access of sympathy for the ungainly figure on the stand. He turns out not to need it, unabashed in face of Mansfield, and despite what he is forced to tell the court. A different kind of moment: the sudden disappearance from her place in the gallery of Patsy Power, a sister of Billy Power and one of the strengths of the relatives, but now for the moment unable to take the recital of events of thirteen years ago again. Other relatives are there, but Kate McIlkenny, the strongest of all, looks particularly forlorn with Patsy gone.

The evenings outside the courtroom are dark now, as we emerge soon after four o'clock each day. There is a kind of loneliness out there too, for media interest has dwindled and only a handful of reporters await the latest comment. Daily a different story about when it will end, the teller invariably citing the best possible authority. The truth is that no one knows, not even the lawyers, who on either side will be trying to get the most out of final submissions.

'Floor three, innit?' says the man in the lift. 'Seen you about. I work here. The gents and that. If you ask me, mate, the judges isn't going to let those blokes out. It's their own kind put 'em in, innit?'

I'm not your mate. Mate.

DAY TWENTY-EIGHT

The end, when it comes, is abrupt. Michael Mansfield has rehearsed the main lines of the men's case, has again underscored the unreliability of the scientific evidence especially; and then he asks the court to allow these men 'the justice of which they have been deprived'. It is 12.18 p.m. on Wednesday, 9 December 1987.

Some points at issue between Richard Ferguson for the men and Igor Judge for the Crown remain to be resolved, and Mr Judge, as he is on his feet, offers the thanks and best wishes of all to the lady assistant registrar, whose invaluable help this court is apparently no longer henceforward to enjoy. In this he is joined by the Lord Chief Justice, who thanks also counsel and court staff for the way in which they have carried out their onerous responsibilities. Lord Lane announces that judgment is reserved and says that it will not be delivered this term. 'Let the men go down,' almost casually. The lady usher delivers her line, 'Court rise.' It is 12.30 p.m.

In the twelve minutes since Michael Mansfield concluded his submission there has occurred a change in the demeanour of the men and their families, almost unbearable in its poignancy. For it has only very slowly dawned on any of them that the talk in court has no longer anything to do with them. There was no break between Mansfield's final plea and the subsequent business, nor any perceptible change of tone or pace. The men look somewhat dazed, the people in the gallery utterly bewildered. As the men go down, one of the relatives begins to sob. It is time to stop observing.

'WRAGG IN CUSTODY'

The final melancholy sentence of a newspaper report of a child murder by the unmarried mother, a girl called Wragg; a report which moved Matthew Arnold to bitter criticism of nineteenth-century British complacency, and a sentence which provoked a particular comment: 'And the final touch – short, bleak, and inhuman: *Wragg is in custody*. The sex lost in the confusion of our unrivalled happiness; or (shall I say?) the superfluous Christian name lopped off by the straightforward vigour of our old Anglo-Saxon breed!'

The use of the surname in the case of a convicted person is a convention still in these islands and perhaps one shouldn't make too much of it. When someone has been convicted of twenty-one murders, the way in which he is referred to in court is doubtless among the least of his troubles. Yet the style is wrong and betokens a wrong stance. It was strange to hear one of the Crown lawyers apologise for referring to a solicitor as 'Curtis', going on immediately to speak of 'Hill' and 'Walker'. The same lawyer mispronounced Hugh Callaghan's surname each time he used it.

THE GOOD GUYS ARE CALLED 'MISTER'.

The confidence of privilege has not been greatly shaken since Arnold's time – and this is true, of course, not only of privilege in England. One of the first things to hit home in those days in London is the precarious state of the notion of equality. An observer is more equal than a relative, to adapt George Orwell; and everyone is more equal than Callaghan, Hill, Hunter, McIlkenny, Power and Walker. If you're Irish, you're not *quite* equal, for all that is done and said. At least the way things are going now.

One of our senators (on the basis, as I remember, of less than a day's visit to the hearing) thought fit to lecture the nation on the perils of partisanship. Thank you, sir; but for you we should all have fallen prey.

It was impossible to be around for any length of time and, out of elementary nature, not to take sides; though in a much more complex sense than that envisaged by the worthy senator. For it was eventually impossible to fail to face the fact that it was people of our own that were on trial and that their judges were strangers to all of us.

'MIND THE GAP'

Said the Tannoy at Moorgate station over and over again, and I heard it twice a day. The gap between the platforms and the train. The gap between the two peoples. The gap between the classes. The gap between the judges and the men.

One Saturday morning, I went to St Paul's and did the usual round. Dr Donne, rake and divine, was in his place, and I thought of some of the poems and sermons. Aren't they part of my heritage too? Then what about Daedalus' musings: how different are the words *home, Christ, ale, master*, on his lips and on mine! A Eucharist was in progress and I stopped to watch. It resembled ours, our old Mass even, and it induced, briefly, a sadness. Another gap.

That was the day before Remembrance Sunday.

People were saying that the judges were biased; others, forgetting Denning, were appalled at such a thought. So are they all, all honourable men.

Were the judges biased? Not wittingly, not with malice; but yet inevitably. A man who is driven to his work is not likely to know how *natural* it is to change your mind about a departure time if your purposes are as well served by a later train. An Englishman, even if Catholic, is probably unable to see the outright ineptitude of the suggestion to an Irishman that money collected with the aim of travelling to a funeral ought instead to be given to the widow. And in Ireland you *can* go to a funeral without thereby endorsing all or any of the beliefs of the deceased. Look at the attendance at the funeral of Seán MacBride. (On second thoughts, that won't be regarded as a good example.) I can multiply instances of the 'culture gap' from the transcript of the hearing.

THE JUDGMENT

This time it is Court No. 2, a maximum security court, I'm told. A huge turnout of media now again, including the man from the *Star*, who thinks the case is about these six IRA blokes going to a dinner dance in Belfast, right? Last night at the Irish Centre in Camden Town some of the relatives said that they couldn't face the strain, but some have changed their minds, and most of the reliables are there. The Bishop of Derry is back, the man from Amnesty, this time a different American, the politicians, constant and otherwise, the priests from the emigrant chaplaincy, Sister Sarah. Lord Gifford, Richard Ferguson and Michael Mansfield are there, of course; and it is somehow reassuring to meet again the still presence of the remarkable Gareth Peirce.

'Court rise', and it does again, and the Justices file in again, and we all sit again as before. Again there is a slight delay and then the men enter. The tension is intolerable. This time they do not have to sit in alphabetical order. The court registrar announces the nature of the proceedings, and Lord Chief Justice Lane commences the reading of the judgment. 'This is a reference by the Home Secretary under section 17 (1) (a) of the Criminal Appeal Act 1968. It arises in the following circumstances.'

It was a sentence about James McDade ('That name is a recurring theme in the history of these events'), spoken within the first two minutes of the judgment, that somehow made me sense the outcome. At 10.16 a.m. one of the lawyers looked across and, barely perceptibly, shook his head, and it was clear then that the men's case was lost. The reading continued, shared by the judges; there was a break for lunch and we resumed at 1.45 p.m. I forgot to make a note of when the reading finished, but it was around four o'clock.

In the course of its judgment the court rejected the submissions of the appellants' counsel in virtually every particular. The evidence of each witness concerning the men's treatment by prison officers and by police was dismissed. The evidence of the independent forensic scientists was discounted. And, incredibly, Dr Frank Skuse was vindicated.

The rejection was total. It was also harshly put. Not only did the judges reject the evidence of two prison officers who spoke of the men's treatment at Winson Green, they went on to express regret at having allowed these witnesses to be called at all. They were not content to point to the obvious problem concerning a witness who admits to having given perjured testimony, but pronounced her unworthy of belief, and said that if forced to choose between her first and second appearances they would choose the first. Not content, at the end, with the conclusion that the trial court verdict was safe and satisfactory they left it to be understood that the Home Secretary should not have referred the case in the first place. They gave their judgment in terms of unshakable confidence.

'I beseech you in the bowels of Christ, think it possible that you may be mistaken.'

EPILOGUE

How can they have dismissed so totally the story of the prison officers? Whence their confidence that they have judged Mrs Lynas aright? And have they really vindicated Skuse, on whose testimony even the Crown counsel seemed to have given up? Legal perspective can hardly be so different from that of common sense. What will happen now?

> *Of what use is my weeping?*
> *It does not carry a surgeon's knife*
> *To cut out the wrongly multiplying cells*
> *At the root of your life.*
> Stephen Spender

We left the courtroom and headed into the darkness.

What right had I, or others of the observers, to persist in questions or give voice now still to doubt?

The answer, even legally, is simple: if a judge may take the role of juror so may I. And with more right. For if a man of law were being tried, his jury could not be all men of law. At the Old Bailey this winter an ancient justice system was on trial. Almost any observer was a likelier juror than the Lord Chief Justice and his associates. And we were left in our unease.

Campaigners for justice for the Birmingham Six soon resumed their efforts to have the men's innocence established. Fresh evidence came to light which revealed grave irregularities in the police handling of the case, including the fact that statements by the men following their arrest had been altered and falsified; and the forensic evidence was entirely discredited by a team of five scientists appointed by the Home Office. In August 1990, the British Home Secretary again referred the case to the Court of Appeal. On 14 March 1991, the Court quashed the men's conviction and – in the seventeenth year of their imprisonment – they were released.

Acknowledgements

Chapter 1, 'Was I Right?', originally appeared in *The Furrow*, 2001, Vol. 52. Reproduced here with permission.

Chapter 2, 'Can Gay Men Be Priests?', originally appeared in *The Furrow*, 2006, Vol. 57. Reproduced here with permission.

Chapter 3, 'Four Half-Truths and a Lie', originally appeared in *The Furrow*, 2005, Vol. 56. Reproduced here with permission.

Chapter 4, 'Child Sexual Abuse: Some Rules for the Debate', originally appeared in The Furrow, 2003, Vol. 54. Reproduced here with permission.

Chapter 6, 'Human Rights and Christian Faith', originally appeared in *The Rights of the Child: Irish Perspectives on the UN Convention*, edited by Pauline Berwick and Margaret Burns and published by the Council for Social Welfare, 1991. Reproduced here with permission.

Chapter 7, 'Christian Values in a Pluralist Society', appeared first in *New Century, New Society: Christian Perspectives*, edited by Dermot Lane and published by Columba Press, 1999. Reproduced here with permission.

Chapter 10, 'Aquinas, Morality and Law', appeared first in the *Irish Theological Quarterly*, 1990, Vol. 56. Reproduced here with permission.

Chapter 11, '"Wragg is in Custody": A Court Case Observed', originally appeared in *The Furrow*, 1988, Vol. 39. Reproduced here with permission.